Five Old Guys

Bindle. noun, may descend from the German word, "bündle", meaning something wrapped in a blanket and bound by cord, for carrying personal possessions (cf originally Middle Dutch, bündle), or may have arisen as a portmanteau of *bind* and *spindle*.

    Bindle is an anachronism linking the miseries of today's homelessness to a Norman Rockwell painting on the cover of the September 20, 1958, Saturday Evening Post, gently romanticizing the idea of life on the road.

    A *bindle* is a bag, sack, or carrying devise, stereotypically used by the American sub-culture of hobos. The *bindle* is colloquially known as a "blanket stick," particularly within the northeastern hobo community.

DONALD H. GEAN

NEWMAN SPRINGS PUBLISHING
320 Broad Street
Red Bank, NJ 07701

First originally published by Newman Springs Publishing 2020

ISBN 978-1-64801-271-6 (Paperback)
ISBN 978-1-64801-272-3 (Digital)

Printed in the United States of America

To Carl Kaales-
Good friend who
inspired The Corn
Caucus, changed the
world.

[signature] 1/21

This little book is dedicated to Ray, Ray,
Charlie, Charlie, and George all of whom died

at home.

Character sketches by Meghan McDunnah
mcdunnah.illustration@gmail.com

Prologue

It's been over three decades now, and the thousands of funny, sad, inspirational, and tragic stories of people who were once homeless in Alfred, Maine, still ricochet through my mind like a BB in a beer can. I remain amazed that this ever happened in the United States and mad as hell that it continues. An old friend of mine, who used to smoke a lot of dope and shoot people from his half-track in Vietnam, once mumbled, "It's hard to shoot 'em when they're lookin' you in the eye." With this collection of stories, I hope to bring a few of my friends up close enough so everybody can look 'em in the eye."

I'm not a very good writer. I'm not. I admit it. So, for those of you who've begun reading this to perhaps find that out, you don't have to bother. If you stole the book, return it—no harm, no foul. For those precious few of you who bought it and kept a receipt, there's a fair chance you can get your money back.

If I were a good writer, it wouldn't have taken me over thirty years to finally pull this much together. I'd have a publisher with a fancy address and would spend the next thirty years rewriting the damn thing to please them. I also would have cashed a check or two given to me as a material token of their belief that I might eventually amount to something they could make some money off of. No checks have found their way to my mailbox.

One of my literary heroes has always been Ernest Hemingway, who once wrote that his goal in writing is "to write one truly honest sentence." That line has always intrigued me while trying to write, but I think I've got it now. I have written one "truly honest sentence," in declaring "I'm not a very good writer." That, then, somewhat perversely, might just mean—what? Who the hell knows?

I've always wanted to be a good writer though, having early on read things like "the pen is mightier than the sword," while sensing there are simply too many things wrong in the world to just let them slide on by. I've worked hard to become a pretty good storyteller; however, believing that if you're not a good storyteller, you ought to write summaries for the *Federal Register* or press releases for elected officials who are down in the polls. But you should not try to write anything of value.

To become a better writer, I even served about six years at a couple of different universities and found that if you hang around long enough, there's a chance you might someday graduate. I did that and actually enjoyed most of the literature courses. One I especially enjoyed was taught by Arizona State University professor Dr. Richard Landini entitled "Formalistic Literary Criticism." That has always been a mouthful even on the 107-degree day I signed up for it as a last-ditch effort to make the five PM early registration cut-off time.

I stood in that line for two and a half hours in heat so overwhelming, three women collapsed and were unceremoniously carted off. There were four lines, stretching across the several acres of concrete alongside the Hayden Library, with hand-printed signs taped to orange road cones, designating which line was intended for a particular course. Whomever the genius was who set those in place ought to be drawn and quartered, since when I finally got to the front of the line, the woman in charge barked, "What the hell you think you're doing? This is the women's PE locker assignment line. You ain't gonna get one."

At four minutes to five, I dove into the only aisle in which there were no people, quickly signing-up for what turned out to be the seminar entitled "Formalistic Literary Criticism." As an almost senior, I had just dropped into a graduate seminar crammed full of master's and doctor's graduate students intent on impressing Dr. Landini with their vast knowledge of literary criticism, research they were involved in counting more commas in Shakespearean verse, and their eminent qualifications to serve as one of his graduate assistants. I, on the other hand, joined this goofy band in an effort to get in out of the heat and to plug a four-hour elective credit hole needed to get my BA in English. Not feeling a whole lot of pressure, I was on track to actually enjoy learning something.

And I did. I learned, most of all, how to read. Not just to organize and verbalize the phonetic cues prompted by clumps of letters, a task I'd mastered back in elementary school, but to think through those clumps, working to understand whatever it was the author was trying to say.

Knowing a great deal about the author's personal life, temperament, culture, society, psychology, sex life, and the times are all methods by which many try to determine how the piece of literature is informed. With these tools, one can argue that when Robert Frost wrote, "I've promises to keep. And miles to go before I sleep," he foreshadowed a coming of death. From a formalistic criticism perspective, we hear Frost's response to that question during a university lecture years after "Stopping By the Woods On a Snowy Evening" was published. Frost said, "No, it was late and cold, we were still a long way from home, I was tired, and so was the horse."

With that in mind, and if I have succeeded at all in telling a few good stories about some of the brave people who were homeless in Alfred, Maine, between 1985 and 2015, your mind might paint you an image of Arthur, peeking out the cellar window, hear the sound of a door bouncing off Arnold's head, and help you quietly smile knowing that Paul died sober—at home. And most of all, you might have a little better feeling that we all have a lot more in common than we sometimes think.

All of these people are real, some still living, and some not living, but who have living family members. In an effort to avoid the possibility of embarrassing any of these good people, I have intentionally attempted to disguise their identity with name changes and other descriptors, which might obviously identify someone. I have asked for and received permission from a few of those still living to publish their stories but have chosen not to use real names, nonetheless.

Five Old Guys

Dead, John looked just about as bewildered as he did alive. The only apparent differences were that his nose wasn't running, and the dark-gray suit I helped him pick out at Goodwill made him look uncomfortable as hell. As I stomped in from the slushy road, the two men and a woman sitting in the little waiting room stood up and the older man asked if I was Don. I admitted I was as he explained he was John's nephew, Claude, then introduced his daughter and her husband. He said John had called him a few years back and told him he'd been at the shelter for quite awhile, but now had his own room, was being treated pretty good, adding, "Don's the boss and makes sure nobody messes with me."

I thanked them for coming and began telling them how important John had been to establishing a real living and meaningful mission for the agency and how sad it was that John was the last of the original Five Old Guys. It was obvious he had no idea what I was talking about and sheepishly admitted that he'd not been very attentive to his old uncle over the years, which would probably bother him a lot in the years ahead. "It's kind of like with Uncle John," he explained, "as the mills closed, you had to move on and scramble to find work. The only thing stayed the same was the goddam bills. There just warn't time to do the things you'd done otherwise." His chin quivered, his eyes clouded up, and he softly added, "I hope Uncle John's finally at peace."

"I think John's been at peace for quite awhile now," I said, adding, "I doubt if you know all this, but he was already at the shelter when I arrived back in 1985 and hasn't had a drop to drink for over twenty years now."

"You don't say. We never knew where he'd gone. Last we knew he was sleeping behind the old tannery here in Somersworth, then when we didn't hear anything for quite awhile, we figured he'd probably died in a jail or hospital somewheres. When he called that time, I couldn't believe it was really Uncle John."

About this time, his daughter said they had to pick the baby up from the babysitter, that it was nice to meet me, and they sure appreciated what we'd done for their Uncle John, gave me a hug, and off they went. Claude sat back down after giving his daughter a kiss on the cheek and started to ask questions about the shelter, the people there, what his old uncle had been doing all these years, and what I meant about the "Five Old Guys." "Was John one of these guys or what—what's that all about?" he asked.

At five o'clock, it was pitch dark, still snowing, and I was certain supper would be finished by the time I made it back to Alfred. I told Claude I'd seen a cafe down the block when I drove in, and if he wanted, we could walk down to it, get a sandwich, and I'd be happy to fill him in on any questions he had about John and the shelter. He said his wife had been gone for five years now, and try as he might, he was still surprised at what a lousy cook he was. We walked over to John's casket and each patted his Goodwill-clad shoulder and then slushed our way down the hill to the cafe.

Over the next four hours, Claude revealed he was a recovering alcoholic with fifteen years sobriety and had known a number of people through AA who had done well at the shelter. He had always wondered what it was all about, but never had the chance to visit. When he got the call that John was there, he vowed to make it over to see him one day, but unfortunately, never did.

Claude was a friendly, thoughtful, and inquisitive man, and it was a genuine pleasure to tell the story of how the York County Shelter Programs came about, the need for such a program, and how it was we were able to craft a five-million-dollar poor people budget out of the leftovers of the conventional human services industrial complex. Although I never saw Claude again, it was on that slow snowy drive home that I decided to someday find the time to write a few of the stories about the thousands of courageous poor people who ended up homeless in Alfred, Maine.

John, John, Louis, Louis, and Paul

In the beginning, there was John, John, Louis, Louis, and Paul. These five old guys came and went during those early years, always returning in worse shape than when they left. They'd each been in the shelter for from one to three years, came in their mid-to-late-sixties, each having numerous public intoxication arrests, and most having been hospitalized in the State Mental Health Institutes. All had been fully employed and housed for most of their lives within a thirty-five-mile radius of the shelter. That was an eternity ago.

Five old guys in their late sixties to early seventies, are sitting around an old wooden pedestal table, covered by sections of old newspapers, ashtrays, and mongrel coffee cups. There are no long butts in the ashtrays.

John One is about five foot eight, 280 pounds, mostly gathered around his belly. He has a blockhead, covered with greying black hair combed straight back, bushy eyebrows shading his dark brown eyes. He sits in an aggressive leaning forward, hands on his knees posture.

He has deep vertical creases along the sides of his mouth, accompanied by deep "crow's feet," radiating out from the corners of both eyes. His nose has been broken numerous times over the years, made obvious by its position a little left of center. He has been a violent man all his life, especially since coming home from the Korean War, which left him forever changed.

He usually wears a lined blue denim jacket, plaid shirt, blue jeans, and heavy leather boots. He is always neat, with hair combed, and his attire clean and not rumpled. Although he smiles most of the time, it is a smile that is more unsettling than just nice.

John Two is a bit over six feet tall, about 180 pounds, with a narrow and longish head covered by still mostly dark wavy hair. He was probably a handsome young man, but one who would never have carried his head high due to his skittish timidity belying his lack of self-confidence. He's now in his mid-to-late seventies, has bushy graying eyebrows, stooped shoulders, large heavy hands with long gnarled fingers brutalized by decades of hard work in the woolen mills, and maintains a subtle smile designed to let people know he is a threat to nobody.

He's usually pretty rumpled, not well groomed, with his hair mussed up, collar rolled under, and his jeans looking like he slept in them, which he often did. He's not dirty, just rumpled. He'd be sitting back in his chair, one long leg crossed over the other, with one hand cupping his chin, and its elbow resting on the other arm lying across his lap.

On his eighty-second birthday, he will begin crying almost uncontrollably when the staff surprises him with a birthday cake. When he's finally able to explain what he's crying about, he'll miserably announce that the only other birthday cake he was ever given was "from my dead wife. I miss her."

Louis One looks older than he is since his stroke. It left a little paralysis on his left side, causing him to drag that leg some, and he's lost about half the use of his left arm. Consequently, that side of his face is paralyzed, causing him to slur his words, while a trickle of spittle endlessly courses down the side of his chin. He spends a lot of time dabbing at it with a handkerchief, which frustrates him a lot since he'd always been a bit of a dapper dresser as a young man, and now hates being forever disheveled.

He is gay, and chronically alcoholic, and grew up in a town that now pays the shelter to "keep him the hell out of town!" His drinking brought him to a place where he would routinely get drunk, harass the tourists for money, drinks, or prostitute himself, ending up in jail or the emergency room.

He has a full head of thick white hair combed to the side, but not well, and no teeth, so that he often places his hand over his mouth in an effort to hide that wretched fact. He is slightly built, wearing light colored shirts and pants, never quite getting the shirt fully tucked in on the left side. Louis sits with his elbows on the table, both hands folded together, with his mouth and chin braced behind them.

Louis Two is tall and slim, and usually smiling so much you might think he's a little "simple minded," and he probably is a little. He's a guy who never failed at anything because he never competed at anything. He simply accepted whatever leftovers came flipping off the table, smiled, and was left alone.

His clothes are always clean, even pressed, and colorful, though not in an outlandish sense. Just pleasantly colorful, with a belt, shirt tucked, and shoes usually polished. He wears dark rimmed glasses and has all of his own teeth, which are in good shape.

He's about sixty years old, the youngest of the five, and parts his combed hair on the side. He'd be sitting with both elbows on the table supporting his chin, smiling broadly and looking to the side at John One, the dominant one, to make sure he stays out of trouble, or could see it coming.

And Paul. He is in his late seventies, short and now thinnish, though once muscled, who fought as a welter-weight back in the 1950s, and as evidenced by his flattened nose and scarred eyebrows, wasn't very good. He has a thin perpetual grin, which makes him look sneaky as hell, but is actually symptomatic of the head trauma he suffered from a lifetime of fighting.

In addition to his late stage alcoholism, Paul is diagnosed with Obsessive Compulsive Disorder, and spends half his time washing his hands, straightening his collar, tucking his shirt in, wiping forever dirt and lint from his shirt front, and emitting a sort of giggle when spoken to. He rarely speaks in sentences, usually little giggle noises, or one-word responses to questions. He'd be sitting at the back of his chair, with his hands folded in his lap, leaning a bit forward over them, with his head tipped slightly forward as he peers up and around to see what's happening. Paul is always neat as a pin, and it is uncomfortable for him to sit next to these guys even though he has known them for decades.

York County Shelter Programs, Inc.

The York County Shelter Programs, Inc. grew out of an earlier community agency named the York County Alcoholism Shelter that was located in the recently condemned old County Jail in Alfred, Maine. This all took place in the wake of many states' enactment of decriminalization of public intoxication laws in the name of more humane treatment for people who suffered from alcoholism. On the one hand, this was viewed as a major step forward in our efforts to treat alcoholism as a "disease," versus just a run-of-the-mill moral problem.

On the other, and more practical, hand this move took away the only safe place poor drunks could ultimately count on to keep from freezing to death in Maine woodlots, village roadsides, and alleys of the few cities large enough to have them. The police no longer felt secure in picking up drunks in public and letting them "sleep it off" in one of the town holding cells. More and more news stories were soon lamenting the fact that a growing number of people, well known to the local police, were found floating in the city harbors and frozen to death in village parks and woodlots.

The Town Fathers shook their heads and demanded the state do something. The state leaders *kerfluffled* and *beshawed* and said it was the responsibility of the Towns, and the mental health community launched a massive research project to determine how much money they could make off this newly "diseased" population. And nothing changed.

Fortunately, the recovering community that lacked money, organization, and mental health credentials soon banded together in the York County area, and across the nation, to find places to bring their brethren in from the cold. A group of fifty-six recovering alcoholics, their family and friends, and a handful of community leaders signed the incorporation documents necessary to create the York County Alcoholism Shelter on January 2, 1979. The old jail came with steel bunk beds, a cook stove, sink, and several office chairs.

Fred pitched in $150, Helen's kids came up with $36, and a $10,000 federal work slot was soon captured and turned into the director's salary.

The early years were pocked by one skirmish after another between the town and the shelter, as the town struggled to understand why "those" people were roaming free throughout one of the most picturesque villages in all of New England.

A steady stream of worn looking people shuffled from the Old Jail up to the Country Store in the Village Center to buy cigarettes and junk food, much to the chagrin of a few locals who believed they should learn to save their meager funds and invest more wisely.

They argued that if "those" people had enough money to spend on cigarettes and junk food, then they could find the money to pay for rent and buy real food. "And" they declared "if they really cared, they would get a job and pull themselves up by their bootstraps! By god, I did."

It's not that the good town of Alfred was full of insensitive folks who didn't care because it is not. It's just that they tended to behave like the rest of the country when it came to understanding the killing dynamics of poverty in America: they knew nearly nothing. They did, however, presume a great deal, most of which was wrong. Somehow, they believed that what President Reagan said about the homeless was true when he quipped, "They just want to be out there."

Now, it's not that those words are so eloquent or have a rhythmic literary quality that causes one to scurry about in search of a recording device to snatch and preserve them for posterity. No, it's none of that because as a sentence goes, it ain't much. But the enduring quality of those words uttered by a United States president in the early 1980s became etched in the minds of many Americans because they wanted to believe it.

Many Americans, who have theirs, don't much care about those coming up behind them. As a matter of fact, many fear them because they privately fear "those" people might cut into their comfortable little slice of the American Dream pie, all of which might speak to their lack of confidence in where they're at, or how they got there.

Desperately poor people, the homeless, scare the rest of us to death. We say a lot to dissuade others regarding that fact, but the truth is, most Americans do not like these human beings much because they tend to "mirror" all of our own and constant frailties. They show us all too organically our innermost and rarely acknowledged weaknesses and fears.

Most of us know we're not that far removed from them, and the most effective deflection is to demonize them at every turn. "They just want to be out there," provides us with the pseudo-moral cover to either ignore or condemn them and perpetuates the foolish notion that people really do like "to live that way." But they don't.

Nobody wants to be beaten, raped, ignored, cold, hungry, and made fun of with no place to call home. Nobody. There is good research that has established that the "bad behavior" heralded on behalf of poor people is the product of poverty. Poverty is not the result of bad behavior; otherwise, most Americans would be in homeless shelters from time to time. No child growing up in America, wishing and dreaming about what they would be when they grew up, ever wished they would become homeless!

Daniel

As Daniel drew his very last breath
in the ICU, I gently grabbed
his big toe and wiggled it
back and forth as my puny
way of saying, "Goodbye."
His breath rattled out and
his life ended, but what a good
story he left behind.

Daniel is about sixty, well built,
and once referred to as "the best-look-
ing man in York County." He has
dark hair, combed neatly to the side,
'70s-looking sideburns, a handsome
face that features those many little
spiderweb trouble lines that come
from lots of years of wear and
tear: the ones of knee-walking,
shit-kicking drunkedness.

Having found the freedom sobriety brings, he has been sober for a couple of decades. His brown eyes are extraordinarily clear, expressing a sense of hyper-alertness. Daniel has worked at the shelter for years and acts as though he can almost smell trouble brewing, and when he does, he pounces and removes it. He's not a mean guy but he's a no-nonsense guy who is universally respected by the people who come into the shelter, so much so that when he's on duty, there simply is no trouble.

Daniel has a genuinely warm and convincing smile, always looks neat and well-dressed in long-sleeved white shirts, and casual slacks. It is evident that he both carries authority, and he has been around.

Daniel stumbled out of a late depression hard-scrabble start just across the New Hampshire line, and started drinking just as soon and often as he could. His alcoholism was well advanced long before he dropped out of high school, and finally rid of that burden, he was able to devote more serious time to drinking. Banging from crummy job to worser job, Daniel somehow stumbled into a job that actually taught him useful skills, provided him with health insurance, and paid him a living wage.

He was so impressed with this newfound prosperity that he only drank once a week—Friday night to Monday morning—and managed to hang onto his aircraft-welding job for nearly ten years. During those years he married, had a beautiful daughter, bought a new Dodge Ram pickup truck, and kept to his "once a week" schedule. Eventually, though, Friday began looking more and more like Thursday, or Wednesday, and soon, there just wasn't enough time in the week for welding. All too predictably, the job, family, and a place to live were just blurred memories as David entered into that alcoholic fog from which many never return.

His days and nights were a nasty smear of drinking to pass out, waking up in vomit, pain, seizure, and the terror that comes in thinking that you can't find enough booze to do it all over again. He vaguely knew if he was in town or the woods—alone or with others. He was always surprised that he was still alive, and always wondered if he had hurt anybody. Those days and nights lasted somewhere between a day or two, and a thousand years, but it just didn't matter. Daniel was dying and he really didn't care.

He was surprised to realize he was being choked by his filthy jacket, bunched up under his chin and dragging him across a parking lot and into a car. Then he was throwing up in a place he knew but couldn't name, and someone kept yelling, "Keep it down, or I'll rip your tongue out through your asshole." When he woke up three days later, he was still in the Old York County Jail turned emergency shelter.

Gerry found Daniel in a ditch behind the Agway Store after someone called to tell him there was either a drunk or a dead body in the ravine, but either way, it smelled so bad they weren't going near enough to find out. Gerry barked at Claude to grab his legs, which he hated since Daniel's trousers were soaked in body squeezings.

Gerry made Claude come along since he had been sober the longest, and now he had to pay for his stay. Claude hated Gerry just a bit more than being sober, but was easily intimidated, so he came along. As his grip on Daniel's legs squeezed the urine out of his trousers, Claude screwed up his lip to block his nose and wished he had never even thought about sobering up.

After a week or so, Daniel began the fuzzy business of remembering. He remembered the fear; he remembered the sickness and the cold; and he sadly remembered his wife and daughter. That was the memory that may be defined as "Daniel's bottom," because in the past, it had always featured them crying and scared. At first, he thought they were crying and looking scared because he was so sick and pathetic, and he could drift on out, believing that somebody out there once cared, and if that was so, they might care again someday if he could sober up a bit. That made the memories at least bearable.

But then, as his scrambled egg began to heal, he experienced a sensation he would later try to describe as "ashamed to be living and too chickenshit to quit."

Daniel knew that they were scared and crying because they believed he would hurt them again.

That is the realization, which would haunt him for the rest of his life. It was the place Daniel would go to remember what life felt like when he drank, and it was the major reason he decided to spend whatever was left of his life trying to get other drunks to understand that freedom was the only thing worth living for. Freedom to not be afraid, or sick, or suicidal, or crazy, or covered in feces, or made fun of, or beaten up, or in jail, but mostly the freedom to never again see the terror in his little girl's face when he came through the door.

Quietly, Daniel began his mission. He had been to countless AA meetings over the years and did not like the notion of telling people about all the things he didn't like about his own life, and really didn't get much out of hearing other people talk about all the stupid and sick things they'd done. He'd heard enough to know that most of those people were as uneasy about staying sober as he was, and he was pretty sure he had, at best, only enough guts to keep himself sober. He also knew the answer to the question, "If a drunken horse thief quits drinking, what are you left with?" He had to do some work.

He began to read. He read the *Big Book*, he read the *Twenty-Four Hour* book, he read newspapers and magazines, and even read the backs of laundry soap boxes when he went to the bathroom. He read everything he could get his hands on, and even conned the Alfred Library into giving him a library card. He had a lot of time on his hands and was determined to find out something about whatever was going on with this thing called "life."

Daniel had been living in the woods and alleys and crazy people's squalid little hovels for more than ten years, and now, he found himself living in a bedroom of what used to be the Sheriff family's quarters in the condemned County Jail, now called "shelter." He was in a room with six other guys, all as equally ripe as he was when they poured him into a badly stained and stinking bed. The farting and belching and night screams made it nearly impossible to get a whole night's sleep, and though he was getting healthier by the day, he began to really miss the thought of a clean bed, quiet room, but mostly, a place in which he could feel safe: a home.

One day, Daniel walked into Gerry's office and said, "Gerry, I been here now six months, haven't had a thing to drink, and I spend a lot of time cleaning this place and keeping an eye out for trouble. I'd like a job. If you can't pay me, okay, but what I really want is my own room." Gerry looked up at him like he was a puppy that just peed on the floor, cocked his head, and said, "Throw Claude out of that room across the hall, and tell him you're the new Supervisor. The sonofabitch has been sneaking shit in here for a week now, and I'm done with him. You start drinking again, and I'll tear your tongue out through your asshole. Got it?"

Daniel told Claude to grab his things and the bottle and hit the road. "Gerry knows you're drinking. You want him to come in here?" Claude grabbed his jacket, backpack, and even managed to miraculously scoop up the bottle of MD 20/20 in one sweeping motion as he flew through the door, onto the porch, and away from the wrath of Gerry.

Daniel had a home, a reason for being, and would spend the next twenty-five years practicing his sobriety, while learning new ways in which he could help other miserable drunks find their own sense of freedom. Daniel became the face of the new Shelter Program, and by the time he died in that Cardiac Intensive Care Unit, there were literally thousands of poor beat-up and lonely people who knew they had at least one friend on this earth in Daniel.

There was another person involved in Daniel's growth from Town Drunk to productive neighbor, dedicated human services professional, and all round good guy and that is his wife, Marie, who hitched her wagon to Daniel's team, and the good they did for others over the next twenty years is immeasurable.

Arthur

Arthur had been a butler in the family of Joseph Kennedy, and like a family appliance, he was shuttled from one household to the next as members moved on, moved out, or died off. After all those years, there came a day when his family made the long-awaited move to a new house in a rustic village closer to Boston.

Following long weeks of hustle and bustle and packing and lugging trunks onto trucks and car seats, and amidst a great roar and dustup, Arthur popped his head out of the cellar window in time to see the caravan pull out and disappear down the Plymouth Road. Somehow, amidst the merrymaking and confusion, all family members had finally united in at least one thing—they all left Arthur.

Arthur had been misplaced, overlooked, or presumed settled since nobody seemed to know whose responsibility it was to tend to him. Sensing that something might be amiss, the families "harrumphed" some, shrugged shoulders a bunch, and moved on. For years to come when they gathered for marryings, buryings, or football games, different members would sometimes cock their heads, furrow their brows, and opine, "Where was it dear old Arthur went off to now? Seems I can never remember where t'was." Another might then stop stirring their coffee or dinking an olive for a moment, purse their lips, and add, "Well, damn now. Seems I once knew that, but for the life of me…"

Climbing out of the cellar, and half-amused, Arthur paced patiently around the wide front porch, scooting dying leaves off with the toe of his shoe. He chuckled nervously, knowing the family would find it quite amusing once they realized they'd driven off without him. After the sun went down, he dutifully locked up the main house and retreated to his apartment above the garage. Fixing himself a can of tomato soup, he fell asleep, sipping it as he sat in his easy chair, sure in his belief that he'd soon be startled awake by a honking horn.

As morning broke, Arthur poured the last of his skim milk into the middle of the Cheerios scattered across the bottom of his bowl. He made himself a cup of coffee, dragged a chair onto the outside stair landing, sat down, and leaned back, looking down the road for the family car he knew would soon pop over the rise to retrieve him.

Later in the morning, two local handymen arrived, unlocked the front door to the main house, and began their annual ritual of winterizing first the main house and then the garage. They drained the waterlines and hot water heaters, sealed the fireplace flues, poured antifreeze into the drain traps, locked the windows, turned off the electricity, and put out the trash. As Arthur watched from the driveway, they poked their heads out of the truck, waved goodbye to him, and away they went.

Arthur checked all the doors and windows to make sure nothing had been overlooked, and satisfied, returned to his little apartment. As the sun began to set, he ate the candy bar he'd packed for the trip, then removed his shoes, and slid under the mattress cover with his clothes on to help fend off the coming night chill.

By morning, Arthur began to suspect something must be wrong since they surely would have missed him by now. Who would tend to the many important tasks, which had always been assigned to him? Who would open the house in the morning, check the furnace, order the groceries, set the table, or answer the door when guests arrived? Who would bring the after-dinner coffee and drinks into the living room and study? Who would do the many tasks he'd done for over forty years? Who?

The more he thought about these questions, the more frightened he became, remembering the family's doctor had come to visit him several months back. There was casual talk about some memory issues, but nobody seemed too concerned. He was now beginning to wonder if he understood just what they were saying and if this had anything to do with them driving off without him. He was having more trouble remembering some things, but so did half the family. Nobody ever told him it was a problem or that they were concerned. It was just a part of getting older—too many birthdays and all.

With those ragged thoughts now tumbling through his mind, Arthur began to fret, fume, and imagine all sorts of dark and possible conspiracies. It then occurred to him that maybe the family had not forgotten him at all—they had left him there on purpose. They were through with him. He was no longer needed, no longer a part of the family, and when the house-closers waved "good-bye" to him, it was on behalf of the family. He, like the trash, had been put out. But, unlike the trash, it was not clear where he would end up.

"The sheriff just dropped off an old guy they found sleeping above the garage down by the church.

He seems pretty confused, mumbling things about the Kennedys coming to get him soon. He don't look so good."

Arthur was about eighty years old, surprisingly solid, with a belly divulging his lifelong fondness for good food. He stood about five feet eight inches tall and weighed probably 220 pounds. He had a fairly square head, covered by a wild growth of graying brown hair, thinning on top, but heavy growth along the sides and back. He was usually clean-shaven, with a small version of mutton-chop sideburns, and bushy gray-brown eyebrows running off in all directions. When Arthur talked about his earlier life before his journey to the shelter, his dimming blue eyes would sometimes flash the brightness of those better days.

His clothes were well worn and a bit tattered when we met, but he still wore the remnants of a black vest, covering a white long-sleeved shirt under a green army jacket someone had given him along the way, and a pair of brown corduroy pants.

Following a six-dollar Goodwill outfitting, Arthur came back looking for all the world like an out and about "uptown butler." He had gained a few inches in height, and his chin pointed straight ahead.

As his mind sneaked away over the next couple of years, he became less and less able to care for himself, and that touch of class quietly drifted away. Arthur died absent the fabled "with family at his side," on a pauper's bed in a joyless gray nursing home that smelled of urine and Pine Sol, but he did not die alone. The shelter staff made it a point to visit Arthur every day, including his very last.

Shoog

Shoog," probably short for "Sugar," was a three-legged mixture of beagle and every other dog you've ever seen. Apart from the missing right hind leg, there was nothing remarkable about her, other than she lived in the emergency shelter with a grumpy old Frenchman named John. She was mostly white with occasional blotches of brown and black fur randomly popping up, had a bare spot the size of a bar of soap on her right rear butt, and would only look at you out of the corner of her eye, never head on. That caused her to look sneaky as hell.

I don't think she knew any tricks other than sometimes stumbling at you if you said, "Come," but mostly, she came only if you happened to be in her way. Soon after I met her, I made the mistake of tossing a pork chop bone to her. She was about five feet away from me in the shelter kitchen, and the bone just sailed over and hit her in the eye. She didn't move when I threw the bone. Dogs are supposed to follow the trajectory of thrown food, adjust their stance to allow for instantaneous repositioning, and attack the object as it comes into range. Shoog just stood there, looking sneaky as hell until the sharp end of the bone hit the inside corner of that eye.

She then screamed and ran into the other room where John was watching the six o'clock news with the rest of the guys and flopped down in front of the TV. She continued to scream dog screams, and belly crawled over to a panicked John who was trying to unwedge himself from an old overstuffed chair, spilling his coffee, ashtray, and stack of old magazines as he rose. He gently picked her up, examined the quarter inch cut in her eye corner, and roared, "You poked 'er fuckin' eye out!" Hustling into the room, I quickly pointed out that her eye was still in her head, and it was just a tiny little cut at the corner of that eye, and I was certain that with a little cleaning it would be just fine. Also, that I was sorry, I was just trying to toss her a bone, but she didn't catch it. She just stood still and let it hit her in the head.

By this time, John had pulled his couple hundred pounds of irate self from the collapsed chair and was doing that nose-to-nose type of heavy breathing in my face while spitting profanities all over me, some of which I already knew but the ones in French were new. What I eventually came to realize was that John was screaming, "She's blind, you stupid fuck!" It sounds so very different in mad French.

Monroe

"Outta the way, assholes!" Monroe mumbled as we slid and bumped our way through some of Maine's Best-Dressed Christmas Revelers. We were inside a beautiful church in down-town Kennebunkport, Maine, on the opening night of the Annual Christmas Prelude. Notwithstanding his mum-blings, folks might have remained oblivious to his bib-overalls, red plaid work-shirt, and crumpled rail-road cap, had it not been for the three-inch bloody gauze sponge sticking out the corner of his mouth. He had no idea what the Christmas Prelude was all about, but he was quite certain that he hated everybody in the Church for any number of reasons, but mostly because they looked happy, and he wasn't.

Here was poor Monroe with a mouth full of pain, which arrived just after we stopped along the road so he could spit out two teeth that had just broken off. Monroe and I spent about half an hour carrying huge plastic bags full of bottles, cans, and maggots, from a closet up near the pulpit, through the entire crys-tal-lighted church, jam-packed with merry-makers, sipping champagne, and nibbling on sandwiches so small. Monroe guessed that they must be leftovers from a real meal.

In response to a panicky call from the good pastor alternately pleading for help and threatening us with the wrath of a vengeful God, I grabbed the first person I ran into as I charged out the shelter door. That was Monroe, and we headed off to remove the piles of gar-bage bags full of returnables the church had collected over the summer and fall months to benefit the shel-ter's struggling budget.

The fundraising idea was a good one, except in the middle of it, the fundraiser skipped town with the receipts, leaving an unknown number of collection sites overflowing with a growing pile of plastic bags.

My first couple of months at the shelter was spent trying to find and remove them. The more time that passed, the easier they were to find because the church pastors, restaurant owners, Town Halls, Laundromats, gas stations, and saloons were soon calling non-stop, day and night.

Monroe had just abandoned his gravel-pit home in the wake of a ten-inch snowfall and checked back into the shelter with his half a mouth full of rotting teeth and rampant infections. Soon, the pain-induced yelling and hell-raising was keeping everybody in the dorm up all night. Not once in his fifty-six years had he been to a dentist, although one had come to the emergency room late one night a couple of years ago to pull four or five badly infected and rotting teeth. That landed him in a hospital isolation room due to a staph infection.

That's about the extent of dental services for poor people: when the pain and infection can no longer be ignored, the emergency room might find someone to pull teeth, and even throw in a handful of antibiotics. This goes on until the teeth are all gone. A soft diet is recommended for the duration.

I'm not sure Monroe appreciated the fabled "Magic of Christmas" as much as I, but by the time we horsed those bags out of the church and returned to the shelter, the end to his dental misery was creeping up over the rooftop. As we pushed the last stinking bag into the car, a well-dressed Reveler tapped me on the arm and introduced himself as a businessman from a nearby town, whose business just happened to be one that made—dentures!

He said it looked as if my helper was in need of some serious dental work, most probably including dentures, and giving me his business card, said that if we could arrange to have the rest of Monroe's teeth pulled, he'd provide the dentures, and in the spirit of Christmas, at no cost. I introduced him to Monroe and explained his kind offer, to which he mumbled something close to "Uh…jeez…yeah…thanks."

Shaking hands all around, we drove back toward the shelter, me feeling real Christmasy, while Monroe continued to bitch and moan, finally blurting out, "Yeah, that's nice, but how the hell am I gonna git someone to pull these rotten little bastards?" Refusing to abandon this welcome little blast of Christmas spirit, I said something as inspirational as, "Well, one miracle at a time, Monroe. We'll poke around and see what we can come up with."

At that time in Maine, a drunk driving conviction in York County meant you would spend forty-eight hours in the County Jail, in addition to the fines, attorney, and court fees. It also meant for some professionals, their licenses to practice could be in jeopardy if they answered in the affirmative to the enduring question, "Have you ever been incarcerated in a jail or prison?"

As a funding mechanism, and to relieve the chronic overcrowding in our county jail, some drunk driving inmates were "furloughed" to the shelter to spend their forty-eight hours in our Drunk Driver Diversion Program, thus avoiding the need to sweat profusely while trying to answer that question, and earning the shelter twenty dollars per night. As the executive director, I approved all jail admissions to this Diversion Program.

When I got back, I walked into my office, which I shared with the dishwashing machine and noticed a three-piece suit sitting next to it. He stood, handed me his card, and said he had a client who had just pleaded guilty to operating under the influence, and had been sentenced to forty-eight hours in the county jail. He further explained his client was genuinely remorseful, and had begun attending AA, but the jail time could cause some serious problems with his dental license, so he would like permission to ask the jail if he could be furloughed to the Shelter's Drunk Driver Diversion Program.

"You mean he's a duh...duh...a dentist?" I stammered, desperately trying to not laugh out loud.

"Yes, he is, and a really good guy, who'd appreciate your help with this."

"Well," I gushed, "I think we'd be happy to admit him into our Diversion Program, but with one condition."

"And just what might that condition be?" queried the lawyer looking as if he was about to be mugged in an alley.

"We have a guy here with a mouth full of really rotten teeth that have to come out. A local business-man, who owns a denture lab, will provide him with free dentures, if we can get them pulled real soon. If your client agrees to bring along his necessary instru-ments, medications, anesthetics, other supplies, and pull Monroe's teeth, we will provide the good doctor with a warm shelter welcome, three hots, and a cot for a couple of days."

Fifteen days later, and sporting an exaggerated smile so all could see, Monroe greeted the dentist and the businessman at the shelter door. They had kindly accepted our invitation to attend the shelter Christmas party, and Monroe insisted on serving as their personal host, scrambling for drinks and sandwiches, bowls of chips, and veggie platters.

They were very gracious, and it was apparent they genuinely wanted to be there talking with the res-idents. They were surprisingly at ease mingling with forty people fresh in off the road. They obviously car-ried away with them an appreciation of the miseries of the poor since they continued to attend our annual shelter Christmas parties for years to come.

I walked them out to the porch as they were leaving, and with big smiles all around, the businessman said, "If another 'Monroe' makes it this far, please give us a call. We want to keep helping, if we can. It feels pretty damn good."

Esther

Lying on top of Esther's coffin today, was a piece of white paper on which somebody had written, "People who are homeless need many things, like food and a place to live, but most importantly, they need respect." Dedicated advocates for people who are homeless are capable of gathering housing, food, and medical care to help folks get up off their knees and learn to better stand-alone by helping them find their way through the maze of bureaucracies that tend to hide those resources from them. Only the very best of them are aware of the respect thing.

For over ten years, Esther gave this most important gift to thousands of people who were homeless in Alfred, Maine. She provided this to old men, young women, newborns, and kids tumbling off the school bus with enthusiasm, good humor, and respect, as she served them lunches in our Dining Hall.

During the funeral service, the pastor asked the guests if they would like to say a few words about Esther, and if so, to please come forward. As our Ambassador of Good Will and All Things Good, Marie rose and took up her place behind the oak podium in front of the others. She began by announcing that Esther had spent over ten years caring for the many people who reluctantly came to the Emergency Shelter simply because there just wasn't any other place for them to go.

She talked about how it was difficult for Esther to understand how people could end up so poor they could no longer afford a place to live, and how she struggled to understand why family and friends would ever allow them to end up living on the streets, in gravel pits, and homeless shelters.

Esther was, in all good and noble ways, a romantic. She believed in the unquestionable worth of every human being, as evidenced through her Catholic faith, and insisted that all be treated with fairness and respect. She came to understand that these were great and noble ideals that were too often in conflict with reality and did not like it. She made her objections known and spent many hours insisting that we at the shelter "fix it." We paid close attention to Esther's demands and have done the best we can, but I know for sure that if she were to pop over to serve lunch tomorrow, she'd point out that we still had a lot of work to do.

During her talk, Marie reminded the guests that Esther had been presented with the Shelter organization's highest volunteer honor, the Volunteer Bread Board Award. She explained that a "bread board" award is symbolic of one of our most basic foods, bread, and that it was a physically large enough symbol so that it wouldn't end up stuffed in the back of a cupboard drawer after the novelty wore off.

Knowing that Esther had no idea she would be the recipient of the Bread Board Award, Marie closely watched her as I read through the inscription, ending with, "And this year's Bread Board Award goes to Esther DuMont!"

Esther jumped straight up from her seat without standing, re-landed, and shrieked, "Holy shit!" quickly covering her mouth with her hand amidst laughter and applause from the two hundred guests, including the governor of Maine.

Lenny

When Lenny shuffled into the shelter, he had no expectation that he was going to do anything but die out of the weather. His alcoholism was the price he paid to slow the madness that flung him from one reality to the next in an instant or an eternity. A noise, movement, smell, light, or touch might set him into places the meanest of minds cannot imagine and leave him spinning uncontrollably through the terrors of still being alive.

Alcohol could change all of that. He knew that the two or three hours it took to pass out were far better than twenty-four hours of screaming. Two bad marriages, two lonely kids, and dozens of pissed-off friends and relatives were the sum total of Lenny's fifty-two years stumbling around the planet, and he really just wanted to get off.

Fifteen years later, Lenny is a homeowner, sells his handicrafts at local craft fairs, the proceeds of which he shares with the shelter. He is well liked by just about everybody, and being articulate and likable, he is sought after as a casual speaker at social service events, discussing the many barriers to services faced by low-income people who are mentally ill.

He insists on crediting the shelter staff and Alcoholics Anonymous with his survival and renaissance, noting that what they share is a willingness to accept all of him: even the crazy parts. Having rid himself of all medications, and there were a great many, and mental health professionals, and there were too many, Lenny believes his life is unimaginably good. He knows he is still mad but has learned that his madness is a part of who he is, it can be controlled, and that it is his job to manage it when it comes. He doesn't like it, philosophically opining, "Yeah, but I don't like having diarrhea or the crabs either."

Krystal

If you're lucky and run a shelter for people who are so poor they can no longer afford a place to live, you might get to read the letters the kids in the shelter write to Santa Claus each year. If you're not so lucky, you may have to read the letters their kids write to Santa one distant day. Krystal's letter said, "All I want for Christmas is my own pillow. And don't forget Mommy's teeth. I love you, Krystal."

After seven foster home Christmases, at the ripe old age of eight, Krystal was spending her first ever Christmas with her mother—in a homeless shelter. This was a "test-drive" for Mom and Krystal, and if it went well, the state would allow the reunification to become permanent. All they had to do was find a permanent home, job, day-care, medical care, clothing, and furniture and then they could be a family.

Our shelter program could now provide the housing, furniture, clothing, food, and help with school and day care placements that was only dreamt about twenty years ago when Krystal's mom came here. However, the never-ending cutbacks in poor people medical and dental services meant that Mom would never get a decent job. It was not possible for her to remove her hand from her mouth when talking in a job interview. Even beat-up-down-and-out people have small immutable vestiges of pride that drive them to avoid total humiliation at tremendous costs. They do things like cover rotting teeth with a hand if challenged to speak.

Krystal's Santa letter rekindled a decade's old smoldering fear that one day we would admit into the emergency shelter the child of a previously homeless child. If that came to pass, I had reasoned we'd have to admit that the long hours, bureaucrat battles, scrounging for dollars, and hell-raising advocacy in trying to soften the miseries of being poor was a god damned waste of time. That simply could not be the way this story ended.

Frank and Marie were given copies of Krystal's letter at lunch the next day, and all quickly agreed on what needed to happen. With only a few tears, promises were made, favors exchanged, and everybody got to work.

On Christmas Eve day, we helped Krystal and her mom move furniture, clothing, and supplies into their new apartment. Dr. Frank had just pulled all of Mom's rotting teeth, and the dentures would arrive within the week. When Krystal went into her bedroom, Marie proudly pointed out the pillow on which her hand-embroidered pillowcase proclaimed that this was, at long last, "Krystal's Pillow."

Paul

As if the Gods had, on one boring day, decreed that a purely serendipity act should occur, Paul was hustled from his shelter bed into his first psychiatric evaluation, outside of a jail or insane asylum. He only had to wait about ten years for the evaluation, which is the time it took for the mental health community to figure out how they could bill somebody for it.

During his prize-fighting years, Paul was known far and wide as "the toughest sonofabitch in all of New England who could not box." He nurtured that legacy for many more years as an even less skilled barroom brawler, which permanently scrambled his precious egg. His new diagnosis were numerous and complicated testimony to medical terminology run-amuck and a surprise to absolutely nobody. All highfalutin verbiage aside, and in the words of his social worker, "Paul was crazier than a shit-house rat."

This woebegone attempt to diagnose that, which was well understood, occurred during his eighty-second year on earth, and Paul would die of congestive heart failure in exactly forty-seven days. Paul had never married, was unaware of any kids, and when he was buried, three shelter staff joined the mortuary crew in performing the funereal ritual of pallbearer. They came together to carry his casket from a sparkling black chrome-laced Cadillac hearse to the naked little hole in the dirt where Paul was forever planted.

Paul was born in the storeroom of a mill town saloon, and quickly dropped on the porch of the Sisters of Perpetual Malady, where he stayed until he was able to run away. At eight, Paul was sleeping in alleys, open cellars, coal bins, and occasionally a hooker would let him sleep on her couch. He earned bits of money, running errands for barkeeps and pimps, who later on would support his go-nowhere boxing career while providing him with food and a backroom cot. "I never touched a drop 'til I was ten," he would bellow when being thrown out of saloons, "so I gotta lotta catchin' up to do!"

Ten years before his death, and on the occasion of his forty-seventh admission to the shelter, I, acting on a tip from another shelter resident and dogged foolishness, found and dragged Paul out of a filthy, back alley garbage shed full of sick drunks and junkies, a few of whom were actually clothed. Paul was one of them, and I forced Paul to look me in the eye as I warned, "Paul, here's a quart of beer to get you to the shelter, but if you shit your pants in my car, I'll beat you to death. Got it?" Paul smiled one of those sideways crooked grins where your dry lips stick to your teeth and make you look goofy as hell and then growled, "Fuck you! You always say that shit."

It might have been the psychiatric evaluation, the quart of beer, or the alignment of the celestial bodies, but when Paul died, he had been sober for ten years. Still "crazy as a shit-house rat," but sober and at home.

Arnold

The trust fall didn't go so well. After what seemed like forever, Arnold finally folded his arms across his chest, shut his eyes, and as he began his backward fall into the arms of the four other group members, one of their ankles suddenly buckled and collapsing sideways, she dragged her wrist-wrapped partner away to the floor with her.

The two remaining catchers noticed the collapse of the trust net, instantly turned toward the two as they thumped to their sides on the floor, and Arnold simply made a full-out body slam onto the wood floor. He bounced once before screaming, "You rotten fuckers! Think this's funny, huh?" With uncharacteristically good luck, his head landed in the crotch of the catcher dragged to the floor by the twisted ankle. Good for Arnold, but painful enough for the crotch-slammed catcher to scream, "Oh, shit! Get the fuck off me!"

It took over half an hour for the group members and facilitator to convince Arnold that he should join the others in the next trust exercise. Arnold's paranoia had been at issue all morning as the group struggled to help various members gain enough confidence in them, so they could actively participate in exercises designed to show them that people are worthy of their trust, and that trust is the thing that enables us all to live more peaceful and secure lives. The blown trust fall had seriously damaged the credibility of the exercise, the group members, as well as the facilitator.

Arnold was assured that the trust fall incident was a one-in-a-million calamity that would never, ever happen again. It was totally unpredictable, and regrettable, since it reinforced Arnold's life-long skepticism related to trust. He needed to get back on that horse, and he needed to succeed. All group members joined the facilitator in urging Arnold to shake off the shackles of his past, to learn to trust others, to know he is never alone, and that he is a new man with unbridled confidence in others, but especially in himself. He could, by God, do these things, and move on with a life full of trust and self-confidence. "He is Arnold, a man who stands on two strong legs!"

The exercise was far simpler, and obviously safer since they'd just be lying on their backs on the floor of the darkened room as the facilitator played Ashokan Farewell: an environment designed to promote pure relaxation while realizing one's own personal space in the midst of others. Still a wee bit skeptical but wanting to acknowledge the support and encouragement of the group, Arnold smiled sheepishly as he gently lowered himself into a sitting position near the door, as far away from the others as possible. With the lilting strains of "Ashokan Farewell" gently filling the room, Arnold soon leaned back and settled into a comfortable, ever more relaxing stretch out position on his back. Arnold became so relaxed he was on the verge of drifting off into a creamy warm sleep.

Arnold's comfy little sleep journey into dreamland turned to shit when the janitor kicked open the conference room door to empty the trash baskets and hit Arnold in the head with the three-hundred-pound door. All eyes snapped open at the report of the wreckage, as "Krrbonk" shattered the gentle air, and all bodies leapt to a sitting position when Arnold screamed, "Oohhoofuckme! You rotten sonsabitches, I'm done with this shit. Git away from me, go fuck yerselves, stupid bastards. Ya ain't never gonna have old Arnold to make shit out of no more. Fuck you!"

Before anybody could quite understand what had just happened, Arnold clapped a hand over a growing goose-egg, stumbled through the door, and ran out of the building. It was reported he ran from the group session, back to the shelter, and grabbed a large black garbage bag. Dashing into his dorm room, he threw his few belongings, and some of his bunkmates, into the bag, and sprinted across the field down toward the highway. Nobody ever saw Arnold again.

Beezoo

The Town decided it could no longer afford to support its poor farm, and the last to go was Beezoo. For over thirty years, he had tended the vegetable gardens, shoveled snow from the walks, cleaned his room, and taken his meals in the house dining room. Beezoo was sixty years old and totally bewildered when he arrived at the shelter.

He crawled out of a town pickup truck, hefted his duffel bag onto his shoulder, and walked up and sat down across from the social worker's desk in the front office. As he settled his bag between his feet, he said,

"Why am I here?" as his eyes welled-up and his voice quivered.

The young social worker, not fully understanding what Beezoo was asking, replied, "Well, uh, to fill out the admission forms, so we can assign you a bed, and begin putting together a case management plan."

Looking even more bewildered, Beezoo shot back, "I have a bed at home. Why'd I need another? I live at The Meadows and have jobs there. I cook, I'm a good cook. What's goin' on here?"

The worker, realizing Beezoo really didn't know what was going on and was getting more agitated, said, "I need to get something—I'll be right back," and ran down the stairs to my plush Director's office located in the dishwasher room.

"Hey, the guy the Town called about, he's here, and has absolutely no idea what's going on. I think nobody told him a damn thing, and he's getting more and more anxious about being here. Can you meet with him and fill him in on what's happening?"

From the office door, I could see him nervously scratching his head, his arm, his nose, and shaking his head from side to side. His mouth was moving, and he mumbled what sounded like "no, not here, this ain't right, gotta get out," and braced himself to rise from the chair. When I stuck my hand out and introduced myself, his eyes widened, and he gave me a fully surrendered limp hand for the shaking, saying, "Can you get me a ride home?"

After getting him to walk out onto the porch, I took the next hour and a half to explain to him that he couldn't ever go back to the Town Farm, nobody could, because they closed and locked it up today. There would be no more Town Farm—ever, and we had agreed to take him in until they could all get together and find him a permanent place to live.

"So, why didn't they tell me? I just saw them at breakfast, nobody said nothin'. How come they'd do that to me? Huh?"

Not having a good answer and feeling just about as frustrated and let down as Beezoo, I finally sighed and said, "I don't know. They're just chickeshits, I suppose. But we're glad you're here now, and we'll work hard to make the best of it."

As Beezoo began to relax with the finality of his situation, I said, "Hey, is 'Beezoo' your real name, or a nickname?"

Beezoo wrinkled his forehead and said, "It's a name I got stuck with in grade school, and after all these years, people must still think it's cute, I guess. I hate it, my name is Ralph, and Beezoo is just a take on 'Bozo.' Bozo the Clown, you know, a goofy clownish oaf people laugh at. That's the shit I put up with every day of my goddam life, and now I'm in a homeless shelter. What the fuck?"

As his story unfolded, it became painfully clear that Ralph's life was just a long series of humiliations, teetering with embarrassments, mired in ridicule and the occasional ass kicking. He became and remained in that community, the focus of perennial mockery, as a child, and then as an adult. The only time people didn't make fun of him was when they needed a strong back to do some crummy job or to finagle from him what little money he might have.

He and his parents lived in a town-owned tar paper shack next to the dump where they worked off their dole by chasing down the tons of paper and debris that blew away from the dump into the surrounding coun-tryside. They were not technically "town employees," which would have entitled them to health care benefits, vacation, and a minimum wage. Nor were they techni-cally "tenants," since tenancy would have required the landlord to meet all the basic health and safety housing codes.

No, they were none of those entitled things, they were just three more of the millions of dirt-poor people trapped in the killing misery of poverty, doing whatever they could to survive for as long as they could. Being made fun of was just one of the lesser humiliations that came from living off the fruits of a town dump, but the lack of health care was the one that killed his parents.

When they came down with bad colds, they pulled more woodcut of the dump to buck up the stove fire.

When their temperatures got so high, they became delirious, they took turns setting each other on a chair outside in the cold hoping their fevers would go down. But when they began to cough and choke and turn blue, the dump keeper loaded them all in his pickup and dropped them at the hospital emergency room. Ralph's parents died from bacterial pneumonia within a week of each other. He was eight, was now known to everybody as Beezoo, and was told he could no longer sleep in the chair inside his parents' empty hospital room.

The child welfare folks dragged Ralph off to his first of many foster homes where he fit in just about as well as any other kid who'd always lived in a house out by the dump. By the time he could legally drop out of school, he did, and from that time until about his thirtieth year, he just hung around. He sometimes slept in the school bus barn, town maintenance shed, unlocked cars, covered loading dock behind the hospital, a furniture store basement, and any other place that looked like it might keep the snow off for a few hours.

He was well known to the police who fielded the never-ending stream of calls about his trespassing and became suspect in every missing bicycle, lawn mower, clothes hanging on the line, garden vegetables, and the occasional steak missing right off the grill. He eventually confessed to me that it was not true he had swiped all that stuff: he hated vegetables.

This was a time before Medicare and Medicaid and the Affordable Care Act. This was a time when you either had wealth, insurance, or just went without health care, unless your local government came up with ideas and resources to help provide different levels of healthcare for their poor. Ralph's town had adopted the Elizabethan model of a "poor farm," where some of its poor citizens might find a home, food, clothing, and limited medical care in exchange for their willingness to help manage the community, which included raising their own food.

Hay fields and gardens surrounded the facility, a dairy barn housed the milk cows, and eggs were provided by a flock of chickens eager to please. Chicken and noodles on the menu signaled a failure to please.

Traditionally, the people accepted into The Meadows residence were older, but usually still capable of helping out with different chores. As the early residents began living longer, they also became less able to help with the chores, and the town had to decide whether to abandon the self-sufficiency model or possibly admit some residents who had more work years left in them.

Ralph was given two choices after he was discovered living in the back of the Sheriff's water rescue trailer: spend a little quality time in the county jail with some really interesting characters from away, or apply to become a resident of the town poor farm. He wisely chose option number two, was accepted, and stayed until they shut it down three decades later.

Ralph stayed in the shelter for nearly a year while working with the town's housing agency to find some rental assistance dollars for his housing costs, and the shelter staff helped him qualify for a few bucks from Social Security. During that time, he worked in the kitchen, helping to prepare meals for the shelter guests and the town soup kitchens. He took great pride in his frugality, and never wasting a thing. I stopped by the kitchen to see how he was getting along one day, and as Ralph was telling me about the vegetable stew he was making up for lunch, "I cleaned out the whole damn fridge," I noticed several whole leaves of Romaine lettuce floating about in the stew. When I pointed them out, Ralph proudly proclaimed, "We don't waste nothin' around here, Boss."

Several years after Ralph left the shelter, I watched as members of the local Lion's Club filed through the catered buffet serving line, at the end of which Ralph stood decked out in a crisp double-breasted white chef's jacket and toque blanche, ladling out hot steaming chowder to the Lions as they pranced by. As I approached him, I peered into the great gleaming stew pot, and couldn't help but ask, "Who made the stew?" to which Ralph gleefully replied, "Chez Raph-a-elle, of course, Boss!"

Ben

"Oooooh Nooooo! They're all dead! I fuckin' killed 'em. I fuckin' killed 'em all. They're dead, they're dead, they're fuckin' dead!" Over and over, Ben screamed, yelled, and wailed his awful message as he ran back and forth between the dayroom and the kitchen waving his arms with a look of terror and doom raked across his face.

A few of the guys sitting in the dayroom were chasing after him on his crazy rampage, yelling, "No,

Ben, you didn't kill nobody. Nobody's dead, you're not thinkin' straight. Sit down and listen. It's yer goddam meds. Nobody's dead!" As one of them hopped in front of him, Ben would put an old signature high school running-back move on them, duck, and scramble out behind them.

Ben was just thirty-two, but already had a fifteen-year revolving-door history with the state mental hospital, spelled by bouts of fighting with his brother and mother over his disability check when he came out. When his money was gone, and it all went predictably to hell, Ben would be dumped at the emergency shelter, and his shelter-shuffle started all over again.

His schizophrenia ripped him out of high school, the possibility of a football scholarship, the only path he might ever have had to college. His last day of high school ended during football practice. Ben ran onto the field and into the bleachers clad only in his cleats and helmet, screaming at the top of his lungs for his teammates to help him catch the murderous Ninja Warriors who were scrambling through, and hiding under, the bleachers. They were armed with blood-stained machetes and had just raped and hacked to death every member of the girls' soccer team. It took four sheriff's deputies half an hour to corral him in the girls' locker room, and they marveled at how some people were able to resist repeated tazerings.

I scrambled out of my office next to the kitchen at the sound of screaming and ran into Ben at the dish-washing machine. I grabbed hold of one flailing arm, as a couple of shelter residents muckled onto the other, and they were able to pin him up against the wall long enough for me to yell at him, "If you don't shut up now, the cops will come, and you go back to AMHI! Whadaya wanna do, Ben? Talk or AMHI: you decide."

By this time, Ben was wild-eyed, sweaty, trembling, and scared absolutely to death. His fear was so genuinely real that the two guys helping hold him against the wall were feeling it too. They began to sweat and tremble, and soon, their own eyes welled up as they looked nervously around in hopes that somebody was going to relieve them. The muscles in Ben's arms and shoulders soon relaxed enough that everybody loosened their grip, and soon, he accepted the offer of a chair. The other guys looked as if someone had given them a new lease on life and gently punched Ben on the shoulder as they shuffled on back to the day room.

Although he'd settled down a whole lot, Ben remained insistent that he had, in fact, killed the astronauts on board the Challenger Space Shuttle, and that God was going to tear him apart for that. He continued, as if repeating a mantra, with "they're all dead...I killed 'em—God's gonna' rip me to shreds."

I initially believed this was just another of the psychotic episodes that could turn Ben from an easy-going, slow-moving, and quietly friendly guy, into a scary out-of-control flurry of chaos and loud noise.

Finally, after thirty minutes worth of pleading, I agreed to go with him into the day room where Ben promised I would see the devastation he had wrought. As we entered the day room, Ben began to jab his hand at the TV, yelling, "See? I killed them. All of them. They're all gone! God's gonna tear me apart just like I did them!" The images on the TV were at first confusing, since all that was visible was an exploding white cloud with lots of debris flying out of it. The image of the exploding white cloud kept repeating as the announcer grimly pronounced the violent end of Challenger and the seven brave astronauts who perished in the explosion.

All of the residents and I were stunned, as we watched and listened to what seemed like a work of fiction, unfolding with us in it. Ben continued to take all the blame for the tragedy, and finally one of the older guys, who had earlier declared he was "sick and goddam tired of all the whoopin' and hollerin' and hell-raisin'," finished with, "How the hell could you done that sittin' here in the goddam shelter?"

Ben thought about that for a few seconds, lowered his head, and in a solemn voice said, "I designed Challenger. I fucked somethin' up."

Ben stayed in the shelter and transitional housing for another ten years, as we continued to pressure the mental health providers to admit him into one of their community group homes. Citing a lack of space, inadequate payment options, and finally, blaming Ben for being "treatment resistant," they were successful in keeping this chronically mentally ill person out of the services, which had been built specifically for him..

With an influx of new state mental health money and mounting pressure from the legislature, Ben and a few others who had been abandoned into the chaos of the "shelter-shuffle," were finally admitted into group homes staffed with psychiatrists, social workers, and medical staff who were capable of helping them to manage their illnesses, versus tolerate the misery and disfunction that comes from neglect and abuse.

One of our social workers ran into Ben at a community fair about eleven years later, and reported Ben was in pretty good shape, recognized her, and was eager to tell her all about his room at the group home, some of his friends there, and asked about different people he had known at the shelter. His last words to her as they hugged and headed off, was, "Tell Don I wrote to the president and told him what I'd done to the Challenger, but he didn't write back yet. Tell him to let me know when he hears something."

Jorge

Squeaking out of my message machine, I heard, "Hi, Don, this is Jessica in the Commissioner's Office. The commissioner and I have been talking about a sticky problem we've got, and I'd like to meet and talk with you about it. It has to do with a special department client, and we're really up against it trying to find a solution. We think if anybody can help figure this one out, it's you, so could you give me a call when you get a chance? Thanks, Don."

Jorge was brought into the country twenty-five years ago because he would work cheaper than the local white folks. Between picking fruit and drinking, he became well known to police departments and emergency rooms. Late stage alcoholism, and traumatic head injury resulting from beatings, left him nearly non-verbal, barely mobile, partially incontinent, and unpredictably aggressive. Oh, and he was an illegal immigrant from Honduras, now living in a nursing home that had just been notified they could no longer be paid by Federal Medicaid funds. Jorge had to go. Now, they just needed a place to dump the body.

"Medicaid rules forbid us to discharge a patient from a nursing home to the street, otherwise, he'd of been out of here a long time ago. When you take him into the shelter, he'll take off looking for booze as soon as he realizes he can. Then, you won't have to worry about him, he's on the street and it's the cops' problem," the facility director assured us.

"The guy just pissed his pants," I shot back, "speaks no English, and doesn't know where he's at. He'll die before the cops get hold of him. The hell of it is, somebody probably pays you to treat people that way, huh?"

We knew the department would screw us out of the money and prescription meds they promised if we took him in, just as soon as the new administration took office. We further knew that if we didn't take him in, it was just a matter of time until someone put him on a plane to a place where he'd probably not live long enough to get out of the airport. So, we needed to get ready because once we took him in, he was all ours.

Most of the fourteen meds that came with Jorge were intended to keep him as vegetable-like as possible, which accounted for some of his incontinence, the hallucinations, and his slobbering persona. He was a stoned, nasty shell of a man nobody wanted. And he was all ours.

For three years we begged, badgered, bartered, and bullied any and every advocacy organization we could find to help get him into an assisted living facility where he could live for the short while before he died. Jorge was incapable of making the thirty-foot dash to the bathroom, so we had our maintenance guy put a toilet in the only single room we had in the whole building. We hired a bright and athletic full-time attendant to provide personal care with orders to make sure he was always treated with dignity and respect.

Lacking success in getting any help from the Human Services Industrial Complex, a Plan B evolved based on our knowledge that one day Jorge would require hospitalization due to his many chronic medical problems. Our hope was that the emergency room physicians would know an emergency shelter with a toilet in the middle of the room was no place to treat his many maladies. They would, in an implied blackmail sense, have to mobilize the resources and prestige of the community hospital to provide the care any other seriously ill person required and to find a permanent placement.

In the middle of an otherwise nondescript night, one of our staff called to tell me Jorge began having difficulty breathing, his blood pressure spiked, he became delirious, and the rescue squad was transporting him to the hospital emergency room. The following day was packed with hospital requests to provide them with the pounds and pounds of medical and clinical records we held on Jorge and to describe the living conditions and services available to him in the emergency shelter. We enthusiastically complied with each and every request, right down to a vivid description of the toilet we had installed in the middle of the only single room in the building, accompanied by a graphic explanation of precisely "why" it was there.

Following my retirement dinner, while shaking hands with the good people who had come to see me off, the hospital president, formerly a social worker who understood very clearly the problems faced by the poor, approached me, smiled broadly, shook my hand, and said, "That seems to have worked out pretty well for Jorge. We finally found charity funds to get him into a nursing home. I think he'll be fine now, and I hope your retirement is as rewarding as what you've accomplished here. There is a quote of Senator Muskie's I've always appreciated, and of which I'm now reminded,

'Sometimes in order to get things down, you've got to be a real sonofabitch.'"

I don't know for sure, but given his many serious medical problems, I suspect Jorge is no longer living. I am, however, quite certain Jorge never knew how vitally important he was in testing and validating the mission of our agency.

Skinny Turkey

A few days after Thanksgiving seventy years ago, a majestic aircraft carrier was floated out of the Norfolk Navel Shipyard and went to war. The ship, her brave men, and boys from all across the land sailed right into the history books as they fought and died in the South Pacific helping to end the awful war.

As I looked out my office window one fall day, I saw an old man, slowly shuffling between the dying plants and flowers in the garden next to the food pantry. When I looked more closely, I

saw he was wearing a navy-blue baseball cap with "USS HORNET" embroidered in bright gold thread across the bill of his cap. Knowing some of the history of that great aircraft carrier, I introduced myself to the old sailor, told him how proud we are of him and the thousands of others who fought and died defending this good country, and thanking him for his service.

He seemed pleased that I knew about his old ship, admitted that he's mighty proud to be a part of her brave and fabled history, but strangely acted a bit embarrassed. As we talked, I tried to understand where that embarrassment was coming from, believing that he and the many other old veterans all qualify as heroes in everybody's book.

It became painfully clear to me when I asked him if he came to the campus often to walk around and see the gardens, and he said he did, and that he enjoyed watching the gardens grow from the springtime planting on through the fall harvest. As tears welled up in his old eyes, he looked up at me and quietly said, "God knows I don't like it, but I can't make it without the food I get here at the Pantry."

The thousands of senior citizens, children, neighbors, strangers, working people, and war heroes, who come to our food pantry in the barn up to the Brothers, all have one awful thing in common—they're hungry. What a terrible truth in the richest country the world has ever known. They're not looking for an investment opportunity, they're looking for something to eat.

Claude

A counselor barged into my office looking like she'd sucked down about fifteen energy drinks, gasping, "Pick up the damned phone. Now! It's Claude, and he says he's gonna shoot himself in the head if he can't talk to you. Now! Pick up the phone."

"What the hell's this all about?" I stammered, and she said, "Claude called in to the shelter and started crying and saying he's calling to say 'goodbye' because he got drunk again and can't take it any longer.

He finally agreed to hold off if he could talk with you, so pick up the goddam phone and talk to the man!"

For the next half hour, Claude yelled, cussed, and cried, all the while threatening to blow his brains out, refusing to tell me where he was calling from, but it soon became clear he was calling from his car parked at a roadside pullout someplace nearby. He'd been sober for over a year and bought a twelve-pack at a gas station on his way home from work. He said he was sitting in a rest area, and had two left, but knew he'd end up going after more when they were gone and just didn't want "to go through the shit anymore."

I got him to start talking about the old days at the shelter when he and another client worked for two months to renovate the attic of an ancient shaker building so five old guys could live up there in their own rooms. He was still pretty proud of that and had remained friends with all of them until the last one finally died a couple years before. Since his first stay in the shelter, he discharged himself several times, but always came back, staying from six months to two years. He'd been in his own apartment and job for over a year and seemed to be doing pretty well.

I asked him if something happened to make him want to drink, and he said, "Naw, things are goin' good, but I just keep waitin' for it all to turn to shit again. I thought a beer'd take the edge off and I's only gonna drink one, then hide the rest in the trunk before I got home, but it tasted so damn good, and I was startin' to get that old good feelin' again. But then, I started bawlin' my ass off and wanted to just fuckin' end it."

After a while, Claude stopped crying and raising hell. He quietly asked if I'd come get him since he was tired and too drunk to drive over to the shelter.

He'd earlier mentioned he had a gun in the car, and at one point holding it to his head, which sure got my attention, so I asked him if he did, in fact, have a gun with him, and he said, "Yeah, I got a pistol, but it ain't loaded, so don't worry none."

When he finally told me where he was parked, I realized he was only about a mile away in a roadside pull-off. I explained to Claude I'd come get him, if he agreed to do as I said. He easily agreed and said, "Sure, but what do I have to do?" I told him I was scared to death to come get him or anybody else who was drinking with a gun around, so I needed to make sure he didn't have it with him when I picked him up.

"Okay," I said, "I want you to lock the gun in the glove box with the ignition key, take off all your clothes except your under shorts, and when I pull behind you, I'll honk the horn. Then you get out, walk over to my car, and turn clear around, so I can see you don't have the gun on you. Then, hand me the car keys and get in.

"You fuckin' nuts? Ya want me to prance around alongside the road in my shorts? I told you it ain't loaded, ain't that enough?"

"Claude, I'm a director, not a target, and not about to take any chances, so please do it, and we'll get you feeling better soon, but you're not getting in my car with your clothes on and me worrying if that gun's somewhere in a pocket or something. You do it this way, or you stay there and figure it out yourself."

"Okay, but I sure as shit don't like it none."

"I'm on my way, Claude, but make sure you do it this way, or I drive on, and that means your boots, too."

Claude waved out his window as I approached his car, went past a hundred yards, and made a U-turn coming to a stop behind his old blue Ford pick-up. I honked the horn once, and big Claude tumbled out the passenger door barefoot and sporting a pair of boxer shorts with red valentines scattered all around, looking wild-eyed and sheepish as hell, with a ruddy red blush covering his entire body.

He gingerly skipped his way over to the car, did a lumbering sort of pirouette, and with a look of total disgust, thrust his big arm in my window and dropped the keys in my lap. After picking his way around the car, he hopped in and scooted down as far as possible and said, "Bullshit! It'd been easier to shoot myself."

He reeked of alcohol, and as he hopped in slurred, "So, awright, gotdamit, Sally got 'em fer me last Valentines' Day, so don't start fuckin' with me about 'em."

That was fifteen years ago, and the last time I saw Claude he stopped up to the Shelter to say "hello" to the many people who'd worked with him over those years. He was living with his wife in an apartment, working in the woods under the table for sub-minimum wages, which is how he'd been paid all his life, and sober for four years.

We spent some time reminiscing about the old days there, and predictably, the day I made him strip down to his Valentine shorts and dance around on the highway.

"There I was, in my goddam Valentine drawers, with cars flying by hootin' and hollerin', and you makin' me run around looking like some naked dancing bear nut-job," he howled, slapping his hands on his knees.

Remembering this big hairy lumberjack of a guy hopping around on his tender bare feet, and Big Boy shorts, I joined him in roaring laughter. Afterward, I said, "I don't think I ever told you, Claude, but when I went and got your car, I parked it up behind the barn, and opened the glove box to get the gun out. It was there all right, but it had six thirty-eight caliber bullets in the cylinders. Did you know that?"

"Oh, hell no! You sure? I was sure I pulled 'em all out, knowin' I warn't gonna shoot myself. I even practiced holdin' it up to my head so's to see if I could. Kinda darin' myself. Christ, I could'a got kilt!"

Bobby B

It was a pretty well-kept secret, something that almost never happens in the shelter. Most clients and staff had already finished their lunches, but nobody had moved. Bobby B, sitting off alone in his corner, hunching over a plate of spaghetti, was oblivious to what wasn't happening and unaware that nobody had left the Commons Dining Hall yet.

There's an interesting dynamic at play within the shelter population, one that is at first unsettling and odd, but later seems to make some sense when viewed from the perspective of a group of people who have little reason to trust anybody. They will tell you that every time they've trusted others in the past, they somehow got hurt. They were robbed, beaten up, raped, fired, evicted, thrown out, or made fun of.

Consequently, it is rare that a sizable portion of the population will come together to advocate for, or agree upon, any major issue affecting their environment. Whether it's the quality of food, room temperature, or a disruptive housemate, they will first tolerate an inordinate amount of discomfort before making a complaint. Their best defense lies in their ability to remain as invisible as possible. You can't hit what you can't see.

By the same token, they remain just as reticent to join in a group activity such as social games, a group sing, or community discussions. It takes a very long time for them to trust enough to share in those experiences, which speaks to the reason it was so strangely inspirational to see that nobody had left the dining hall. Bobby B had let it slip to a bunkmate who'd given him a piece of his own birthday cake, that in his whole life, after almost seventy-four birthdays, nobody had ever given him a Birthday Cake. Sitting alone in his corner was not unlike how he'd lived his entire life.

Bobby B had blue eyes that still sparkled and smiled some, even though they were planted in one of the homeliest faces one could imagine. He was not disfigured, or scarred, or maimed in some God-awful way—he was simply homely as hell. He was a meatless six foot three, whose shoulders had long ago surrendered to a gravity, complicit in Bobby B's desire to remain as invisible as possible.

He had a huge protruding nose with gaping nose holes, which ran constantly due to chronic sinusitis. Bobby B some days just gave up trying to stem the flow with toilet paper, napkins, or his sleeve, and wore the troubles on his shirt.

His face was long and narrow with those quiet smiling eyes sunk way back behind cliff-like cheekbones that dominated, as though his face existed above and below a shelf. His arms were long, and his fingers ran from his elbows out beyond reason. They were gigantic, and if he made a fist, it looked like he was holding a spool of logging rope. When he sat on a chair, he crossed one lanky leg over the other, bent at the knee crook, folded his arms across his belly, and with a quick glance, it looked like somebody had stacked a bunch of arms and legs on a chair.

Bobby B spent his entire life taking whatever came along, not asking for much, and getting far less. What he did get was constant brutal ridicule, cots in storerooms, dogs sicked on him, and the worst jobs nobody else would do. He mucked the waste out of out-houses as a boy, and later cleaned saloon bathrooms after they'd been fouled by brawling drunks who took great delight in pissing on the walls, defecating in the sink, ripping urinals from the wall, and vomiting only everywhere.

They'd usually scratch a greeting to Bobby B into the wall paint, saying things like "BB, you ugly piece of shit." Bobby B stayed at that job for nearly thirty years, mostly because the barkeep let him sleep in the storage room and eat the leftover bar food.

There came a time when he could no longer heft the buckets, mop the swill, and shovel out the filth and was fired with no word of appreciation, vacation pay, or the last four days he worked. Stumbling from alley to alley to open garages and the occasional town holding cell, a judge finally suggested he check into the shelter down the road, otherwise he'd probably freeze to death out there.

Crossing the dining hall one day, I heard a piano playing in a room off the dining hall. I stopped to listen, and when I peaked in to see who was playing, I saw one of the homeliest men I've ever seen, playing some of the sweetest music I'd ever heard on an old donated upright piano.

After a bit, I introduced myself and asked him where he learned to play the piano so well. He told me he had a job, cleaning a filthy saloon for thirty years that came with an old upright piano. Each night, after he'd finished mucking out the saloon, he'd sit and play that old piano until the sun came up.

Bobby B couldn't read a note of music, but was one of the best piano players around, which made him the favorite of almost everybody in the shelter. Not a guest or staff holiday, birthday, marrying, or burying, went by without Bobby B setting the tone by taking all requests and making unhappy people feel a little better for a while. That's why nobody had left the dining hall that day—they were waiting for the bakery crew to show up.

It wasn't until the Baker placed the candle-covered cake in front of Bobby B that he sat bolt upright, threw his arms into the air, and let out a happy howl signaling that he understood he'd just been given his very first Birthday Cake. His reaction was spellbinding for all who stood to clap and cheer. Everybody joined in with a full-throated rendition of "Happy Birthday," culminating in congratulatory shouts, and good-natured encouragement for Bobby B to "Make a wish and blow out the damn candles."

By now Bobby B was bawling like a baby, and with a huge smile, he eagerly bent out over the flaming cake and began to blow. To most everybody's subdued horror, as he blew, the mixture of tears and nasal drippings coated the top of the cake, now swathed in smoke and slobber to the point that several guests turned their heads away to gag as quietly as possible.

You could almost hear the communal thought, *How are we going to turn down a piece of the first birth-*

day cake this old man has ever had without making him feel far worse than if he'd never gotten one in the first place?

Fate and clumsiness mercifully intervened as Bobby B tried to rise from his chair, lost his balance, and in an effort to brace himself, plopped his huge left hand squarely into the middle of the smoldering cake, dragging it off the table and onto the floor. A muffled "whoosh" rippled across the room as everybody at once accepted their salvation and began to cheer, and the baker shouted, "Not to mind, we have blueberry muffins, fresh outta the oven, and on their way over!"

After about ten years living in our transitional housing building on the Brother's Campus, Bobby B began to forget where his room was, when to take his medications, and was found a couple of times walking around in the snow with no coat, hat, or shoes. His dementia was moving fast, and soon he moved into a nearby nursing home where he stayed until he died.

I, and three other staff, drove down to see him on his seventy-sixth birthday, taking along a Bakery Birthday Cake. When we arrived, the charge nurse pulled us aside to caution us that he was losing ground very quickly, probably would not recognize any of us, and was mostly non-communicative.

Bobby B was sitting in a corner nest to an upright piano, with his wheelchair turned toward the wall. He was dressed in a blue-striped hospital gown over a pair of surgical scrub pants and slippers. His hair was mussed up, he was unshaven, and his large homely face lacked any expression: it was blank. When we turned him toward us and took turns telling him how happy we were to see him, and how everybody at the shelter sent along their love, and best wishes, his expression remained vacant. His eyes were staring someplace we could not see, and not a facial muscle so much as twitched. Bobby B was gone.

The people who came along were tearfully shaken by the sight of their old friend, and in a last-ditch attempt to see if there wasn't just a bit of Bobby B left, one of them put her arms around him and told him about the birthday cake they baked for him. Another placed it on the table and wheeled him up to it so he could see that it said, "Happy Birthday, Bobby B. We miss you."

We were feeling pretty crummy when we walked slowly away from our old friend as he sat staring somewhere out beyond his last birthday cake. Ending a brief discussion with the nurse outside the door, we were stopped dead in our tracks when we heard the faint random tinkling of piano keys.

We rushed back into the Dining Room, noticing the keyboard was covered in white and red frosting, and glancing over at the cake, saw a huge full handprint in the middle of it. All the way back to the campus, we tried to convince each other that despite the fact his eyes were closed and his head was just hanging down, there may well have been just the slightest scintilla of a smile on Bobby B's face.

Betty

The board meeting had been chattering on for over two hours as different members sparred with staff over the pros and cons of whether to include a private bathroom in each of the eight single rooms we had just been awarded grant funds to build. The additional cost was in the neighborhood of $15,000 more for each bathroom and was not included in the grant. If we included the bathrooms, we'd have to take that money out of the small precious unrestricted donations fund, which would leave us with next to nothing in the fund.

"I could've told you before, I forget if I did," Betty rasped, "but I got an apartment and will move in the first of next month. It's over in Biddeford, close enough to walk downtown and the Shop & Save, and I'm on the first floor. Maine Housing got me a voucher, so I only have to pay about a third of my disability check and leaves me enough for food and my medicine. I'm so grateful to all of you and the people at Maine Housing who helped me do all the paperwork I'd never been able to figure out. It's a dream come true, I never thought I'd end up this lucky. It's got one bedroom with a single bed and closet, a cute little kitchen, they called it a 'galley' kitchen, right off the living room, that's got a couch and easy chair in it. From the window in there, you can see the flowers in the St. Mary's yard across the street." Betty stopped talking for a moment to catch her breath and untangled the oxygen tube from around her oxygen bottle, then continued to rasp-talk in her breathy whiskey voice from too many years of cigarettes and alcohol.

"For the first time in my life, and I'm sixty-two now, I'll have my very own bathroom. In the foster homes, hospitals, group homes, jails, and the shelters, I always had to wait and share the bathroom with all kinds of people usually after I cleaned up their mess. The shelters and jails are the worst. You have to walk away from your bed, and if you leave your stuff there, they'll steal it. If you take it with you, and someone wants it, you could get beat up. I'd go for months without a real shower, would pack all my stuff in a garbage bag, and hold it while I's on the toilet," she giggled, "then wet a towel and take it back to my bunk for my bath."

"But of all the nice stuff in my apartment, having my own bathroom's the best. I got my own toilet and shower. It doesn't have a sink but doesn't matter since I have a big stainless sink in the kitchen I can use. I walked down to the Goodwill and bought a few things to kind of fix it up, you know, and one of the things I got is a little mirror I'll hang on the wall above the sink. It looks good with a pretty metal frame that has some kind of bird as part of the frame top. I just love it."

"Betty, congratulations, and we're all happy to hear about your apartment. We know you've waited a long time. I think ever since you came on the board, if I'm not mistaken, and you're going to be very happy with it, we know," said the Board President, "but I just want to remind everybody of how hard we and the staff worked to raise those non-restricted funds. The spaghetti dinners, raffles, dances, and personal solicitations we made. It was a helluva lot of work for a lot of people, and even though the bathrooms would be awfully nice for those eight people, it will leave us with almost no reserve money, which is where we've always been, and where we've worked to get away from. I'd have trouble voting to do that at this point."

"We know," I added, "from our experience with the other housing we've developed, and in talking with other housing folks, people don't stay for long periods of time if they don't have their own bathroom. The units we have with private baths have almost no turn-over, but those that don't have them remain vacant for longer periods of time. The lost monthly revenue from those rents, soon equals then exceeds the amount of money needed to put those bathrooms in from the start. We'd really like to include them and ask the architect to get us a more accurate cost estimate before the board votes on this."

The president nodded approval and said, "That sounds like a good place to leave this until we see those numbers. Can we get them in time for next month's meeting?"

"You bet we can, and thanks for taking some time to think about this.," I said.

The agency by-laws specified that at least one formerly homeless person, who had lived in the agency emergency shelter, would serve as a member of the board of directors, and it was into this position Betty had been elected two years before. She had come into the emergency shelter six years ago, having walked the mile and a half from the Village Center where her hitchhiking ride had dropped her. Most of that walk is uphill, and when she would talk about that walk years later, she'd remember it as "the most miserable goddam week of my life."

Betty had collapsed on the sidewalk of a neighboring town, eventually picked up, and taken to the emergency room where she was diagnosed with chronic obstructive pulmonary disease, malnutrition, and late stage alcoholism. She remained in the hospital for several days, after which she discharged herself against medical advice. Armed with the address of the Alfred shelter, and stoked with a belly full of good food, and a system bubbling with respiratory drugs, Betty felt well enough to walk the half mile to a convenience store filling station where she propped herself up against a gas pump to ask customers if they were headed to Alfred, would they give her a ride to the shelter there? She got as far as the highway intersection and spent the rest of the day walking thirty to forty feet, sitting down to catch her breath, then walking another thirty to forty feet.

Over the years, we had managed to cobble together our own health care program, including a full-time nurse, weekly medical doctor clinic in the shelter, and ready access to our new and growing community health center. Betty was soon a part of a case management plan, which included a wide array of services, including medical, substance abuse treatment, and housing search, all of which she took full advantage of as an eager and willing participant since, in her words, "I just pissed away my ninth life!"

She stayed in the shelter for about a year until a single room opened up in one of our Women's Transitional Housing Residences, volunteering in our Food Services Program, which included the food pantry and free meals kitchens. During these years, she became known to, and well respected by, all of the staff and many board members, so when the client board member position came open, Betty was the immediate and unanimous choice.

Her room was located six miles from the shelter campus where the board meetings were held, so the board created a budget line to enable her to hire a ride to and from the meetings. They soon realized that although this was a positive and sensitive reaction to her low-income status, it also served to underscore the fact that she was "the low-income board member." I continue to have great pride in that old board for recognizing and fixing that inadvertent bit of discrimination, by expanding the board member travel assistance budget line to make it available for all board members.

Betty was a small feisty woman, with short curly dark hair, and tired blue eyes that darted about as if they were on automatic pilot looking out for trouble. She seemed to never be fully relaxed, always on guard for that inevitable "something." A lifetime of alcohol abuse, and the pure hell that comes with it for everybody, but especially for a woman tending bar in knockdown drag-out saloons, will do that to you. Betty's survival instincts were uncomfortably superb.

Betty was able to finally wrestle her alcoholism to a stand-still, but the damage to her body was significant, and one week before our next board meeting, Betty was taken from her room by ambulance to the hospital where she died from heart failure complicated by her chronic respiratory problems.

Following a few celebratory moments remembering Betty at our board meeting, the president said, "I am so sorry Betty didn't have the chance to hang that mirror over her sink and be able to enjoy having her own private bathroom. It's such an apparently small thing to most of us who can't know what that could possibly feel like, and remembering how Betty described having to hold everything she owned in a garbage bag on her lap when she used the toilet, puts its importance way out beyond 'nice.'"

"Betty helped point us in a direction, that if we hold it, will enable us to know we're continuing to place the physical and emotional welfare of the people who come here where it belongs—at the very top of our priorities list. I suggest we follow the advice of our former board member and friend, so please join me in unanimously approving the use of our unrestricted funds to build private bathrooms into each and every housing unit we create from this day forward."

Donnie

As we lope along from day to day, life can be wildly unpredictable, going out of its way to test just how tightly we are wound, followed by another just to see how quickly we rewind. A never-ending blizzard of things that disrupt the fleeting moments of peace and dependability by which we try to gauge our progress along the path.

As I pull myself into a sitting position, I'm pis-soffedly surprised to see a fresh metal sign stuck on a post where the front porch handrail waited to help me climb the post office steps for fifteen years, read-ing, "Caution No Handrail." Fleeing from the table to throw-up my Caesar salad out of the Sunday din-ner crowd ear-shot, I condemn to hell the farmers mentioned in the news flash warning of E-Coli laced Romaine lettuce. And now I'm two hours late for my first day of work since the second hundred-year flood in two years took out the bridge—again.

These flakes are but an infinitesimally small sam-pling of the blizzard, enabling us to relish the things that don't knock us on our ass, make us puke, or look for work every now and again. As terminally boring as routine and process can be, they are the markers to which we look and cling as we stumble along. Sunrise to sunset, ebb and flow, plant and harvest, life and death and taxes—these are the things we can count on.

And so, it was with Donnie for fifteen years. Thanksgiving at the shelter was an especially busy, happy, and satisfying time for all of the volunteers, staff, board members, and community. Our family had pre-pared and delivered full Thanksgiving dinners to fami-lies, struggling to get by for many years, starting with a single frozen turkey we asked the only police officer in Lisbon, Iowa, to deliver to any family he thought could use it, to a record fifty families the last year it was done only by our family.

Recognizing we could never keep up with the growing need, we were able to infuse into the mission of the agency that Thanksgiving spirit, and during my last year as director, we distributed nearly two-thousand Thanksgiving dinner boxes to area families who were required only to make it up the hill on their own and ask. As regular as clockwork, I could count on our volunteers and staff to begin soliciting food, recruiting additional helpers, and setting the stage for thousands of our neighbors to enjoy a very special Thanksgiving time. I also knew that Donnie would return to the shelter for Thanksgiving dinner and leave once the snow melted.

Working in the woods, yard work in town, and an incredible set of outdoor survival skills had hardened Donnie to the point that he was physically strong, but as the birthdays piled on, and his mental illness increasingly threatened his ability to find and use those skills effectively, Donnie was forced to seek better shelter in the winter and find out how to start dealing with the voices and hysteria of being out-of-control-crazy alone in the woods.

Donnie was taken screaming and yelling into the emergency room by two sheriff's deputies, who'd chased him down in the woods after responding to a complaint that a man was running around town, screaming obscenities and throwing left-over Halloween pumpkins at the passing cars. A couple of weeks later, he was given a ride to the shelter, arriving just in time for Thanksgiving dinner. He was fairly subdued, as would have been a herd of elephants had they sucked down the basket of pharmaceuticals he had on board. He was in his mid-forties and built like a middle-weight wrestler with dark brown eyes and a shaved head. None of that, though, caused him to stand out from the dining room crowd when I peeked in, but what did catch, and hold my eye, was the blue-black-and red tattoo of a giant butterfly, covering the entire top of his head.

I walked over to introduce myself and welcome him to our dinner, to which he thoughtfully listened, and said, "This is some good shit, man." I heartily agreed, sat down, and had a good talk with him about living in the woods, his travels around the country, and finally I had to ask him where he got the butterfly tattoo. Foolishly, I had imagined the story would go something like, "Well, I got drunk up to Portland one night, and rolled into this tattoo parlor where I picked this off a chart hanging on the guy's wall. Another fifth of coffee-brandy and three-hundred bucks later, I woke up with this on my head."

Donnie, however, clearly explained that when the voices started, he was "wicked scared and didn't know how to get rid of them and couldn't sleep. The only time they'd slow down sometimes was when I'd read things."

He started going into the town library and reading all kinds of magazines, often until they closed at night. The librarian, it turned out, was a distant cousin, who kept an eye on him, and one day gave him a "National Geographic" magazine that had a big story about butterflies in it.

He said he spent a whole week reading and rereading that story, fascinated at how "those beautiful tender butterflies come out of such ugly little wormy bastards." He said, "I wished I was a butterfly, so I could do that too. I was tired of being an ugly little wormy bastard. So, I tore out the picture of this one," pointing to his pate, "and hitch-hiked down to Portsmouth and had the tattoo guy put it on my head. How do you like it?." I asked if it helped with the voices, and he snapped, "Yassuh! Cuts 'em way down."

Donnie stayed with us until the spring snowmelt, then headed on back to the hills, returning for Thanksgiving dinner the following year and every year thereafter for fourteen more years. During his winters in the shelter, he spent a lot of time helping out in the food pantry, working in the kitchen, and with different jobs around the shelter. Three nutritious meals each day, living in a drug-free environment, and quick access to healthcare, served to keep him healthy enough to make it through the late spring, summer, and early fall, months in the woods.

Each year, I wondered if he'd make it back and always felt relieved when Thanksgiving rolled around, and I'd look across the dining room to spot his butterfly. One year, I ran for the state senate and knocked on over seven thousand doors, trying to meet the people in the thirteen different town, to tell them about my ideas on issues that might be of interest to therm. It was a clear cool but sunny day in October when I climbed the wide sweeping stairs up onto the spacious covered porch of a stately Victorian mansion in one of the hill towns. The porch swung around two sides of the house, and was probably twelve feet wide, standing over four feet off the ground.

After my first knock on the massive front door, there was no answer, so I knocked again a moment later. Getting ready to leave, I made a parting knock on the door and was startled to hear someone yell, "Are ya dumb, or what? They ain't home for chissakes, so quitcher bangin' on the goddam door!"

It sounded like the voice came from beneath the porch, and I replied, "Who's that?"

To which the voiced replied, "Git off the porch and go away!"

I heard some scuffling underneath, and soon, a red, blue, and black butterfly dragged Donnie into a standing position at the end of the porch.

"Donnie," I yelled with a hint of relief in my voice. "What the hell you doing here?"

"Hey, Don, didn't know it was you, I live here. How 'bout you?"

"You live in this big old house, Donnie?" I asked as I climbed back down the stairs.

Donnie laughed, saying, "Naw, un'er the porch."

He explained that he did yard work for the owners who had headed off to Florida for the winter and let him stay under the porch to keep an eye on the place.

Donnie came over and grabbed me in a big bear-hug, happily announcing it was only about four weeks until Thanksgiving dinner. I explained what I was doing running for the legislature and banging on doors, to which he said, "Hell, Don, I'd sure vote for ya, but I don't vote. They're all a bunch of thievin' assholes, ya know. Oh, sorry, not you, them other assholes, I mean."

And he was right on time for Thanksgiving dinner.

Joey

"I'm happy to see you made it back, Joey, how you doing?" I asked as I shook his bandaged hand in the breakfast line.

"Thanks, it's good to be back. It ain't gittin' any easier, and I warn't sure I'd make it back this time. I came in from the hospital last night late. They kept me a couple days. Passed out and damn near froze to death up to Portland," he said as he held up his bandaged hands to explain. "Got frost bit on my fingers and thought they were gonna chop some off but looks like I can keep 'em all. I gotta quit this shit."

His bandaged fingers were swollen with some leakage from several. It smelled as though he might be overestimating the number of fingers he'd end up keeping, but we'd be able to monitor the infections and get him the treatment needed through the health center funding we'd recently been awarded. It was clear Joey would be with us a while this time unlike the other dozen or so times we admitted him to the Shelter.

During his early years with us, other clients sometimes called him "Joe College" since he usually wore college sweatshirts he got at Goodwill, had a crew-cut, blue eyes, and with his stocky build, looked like a college jock. That was the early years, but now his face was marred by years of drunken fighting, nose busted, eyebrows heavily scarred, and hair scraggly, but still sporting college sweatshirts

Over the past five years, he'd shown up drunk and sick, and we helped get him detoxed, provided him with food, shelter, medical care, substance abuse treatment, and repeatedly developed plans to enable him to live more independently. For as much as six months, he was able to remain sober, always earning the support and respect of staff and other clients for his easy-going and upbeat approach to living in the community structure and helping out with maintenance jobs across the campus. So much so, that during his last stay, there was talk about hiring him as a part of the housing maintenance team if a position opened up. When he took off again, there was a general sense of sadness, but no surprise. After nearly five years, we had hoped and worked and hoped some more that "this time, he'll get it," but he didn't.

"You really don't have to quit this shit' as you know, but you will quit soon because it's going to kill you," I answered, knowing his next statement would be, "Yah, I know, and this is it. I can't take no more," which we'd heard every time he returned. But then he said, "I thought I was gonna die up there and what scared me most was, I know there ain't nobody left would claim my body. Ain't that a helluva place to end up?"

After about forty years, developing and running substance abuse treatment programs, I've come to believe that of all the people who receive treatment of any kind, those who attend AA or NA, find salvation through organized religion, or adopt rigorous fitness regimes, about a third of them tend to get better, a third get worse, and for the other third, it doesn't seem to make any damn difference. One could argue, if my highly sophisticated calculation is true, those are dismal outcomes overall, and that might be true if it were not for the rest of my conclusion. Watching, over time, one would realize those are rotating thirds—as long as the heart continues to beat, and there is still at least one other human being who continues to support the sick drunk or junkie, there is a chance they will one day change that behavior.

When their time is right, the "no damn difference" and "worse" groups tend to swap places, metamorphosing from "no damn difference" to "worse" to "better." If this is true, and I tend to believe it is at least as true as the slick commercial advertisements for resort-style treatment touting outlandish outcomes, the trick is to not give up, unless they are pronounced dead. Denying readmission to a relapsed substance abuser is an institutional convenience, probably prompted by reduced third party remuneration, or provider weariness, and antithetical to the concept of recovery.

Knowing that, when Joey said "there ain't nobody left to claim my body. Ain't that a helluva place to end up?" I heard a major change in his thinking. It has to be terrifying to admit you've alienated everybody you ever cared about to the point they'd pay no attention to your death. That was different: something seemed to be changing with Joey, and his heart was still beating.

Joey settled back into the routine of living in the emergency shelter, working with his case manager to develop a plan to help him live independently, and was soon participating in group and individual counseling while undergoing a series of surgeries which cost him both little fingers and one ring finger. The surgeries were complicated by his overall lousy health, and it looked for a time that he might lose several more fingers. After about three months, Joey was healed well enough to begin working half days with the maintenance team while showing a new and more positive attitude toward his counseling sessions and working with a new AA sponsor.

After a year, Joey was continuing to make major life-style improvements and was hired into an entry level maintenance position. Soon after, he moved into his own efficiency apartment and was able to save enough to buy a used pick-up truck to drive back and forth to work. From all indications, Joey had finally "got it" and was happily on his way to living a peaceful productive life, and everybody felt good.

The fire captain called as a courtesy to our agency to let me know Joey had been arrested for public intoxication, resisting arrest, and disturbing the peace. He climbed out his apartment window onto the porch roof, obviously drunk, and was screaming obscenities at the firefighters in front of the station across the street. When they yelled at him to get down off the roof, he dropped his drawers and mooned them and the gathering crowd.

As the cops were rolling up, he climbed down the porch trellis and took off bare-assed down the street but was tackled by four groomsmen in front of the church as the wedding party was moving out onto the front steps. When the cops caught up with them, Joey was squared off with all four of them, with boutonnieres, bow ties, and buttons scattered all about. They all ended up in the same emergency room with Joey, who wasn't quite through fighting. The cops ended that.

Joey was transported from the emergency room to the county jail where he remained for the next six months. Near the end of his sentence, his probation officer called to let us know when he would be discharged and asked, "Whadya' wanna do with him?"

To which I said, "Is his heart still beating?"

He said, "Yeah, so what?"

"Well, the recovery process for substance abusers should be viewed as cumulative. All the things that happen to them during that process, good and bad, at some mystical moment meld and conspire to teach or convince them that straight and sober is easier than drunk and stoned. It's probable that losing a job, divorce, loss of health, legal problems, financial problems, and all the other lousy things afflicting them when they're using and sick are just as beneficial to their eventual recovery as positive events coming out of it such as a new job, better relationship, good health, and financial security.

"So, send him on back," I said, "we're not done yet."

Earl

On a cold December night a
few weeks after I started at the
shelter, I answered the phone
to hear a woman screaming,
"Earl's fuckin' crazy and if
ya don't come git him we
gonna call the cops on
him, agin. Hurry. He's
fuckin' crazy, yellin' at
people ain't there, yel-
lin' the ceilin's on fire,
and starin' at me like some
kinda sex fiend. I know he's
gonna hurt me. Ya gotta
come git 'em, an hurry!"

Earl was staying in
a one-room summer
cabin near the beach

with his mother and an older brother, both of whom were roaring drunk, taking turns throwing things at Earl, and screaming at him to "Git out, die, don't never come back!" Earl was sitting on a filthy broken-down sofa, covered with dirty clothes, shoes, a skillet, and the squishy remnants of a cheese pizza, they'd thrown on him. He had a wild maniacal grin covering his skinny stubbled face, yelling, "Fire, ceilings afire, gonna fry yer asses. Fire! Ceilings afire, gonna fry yer asses!"

He looked up at me and said, "Hey, Bub, ya here to put out the fire?" I told him who I was and asked if he'd like to go with me to the Alfred shelter before the cops came and he chirped, "Yeah, I been there. They know me, we'll let these fuckers burn to death," and laughed non-stop all the way back to Alfred.

It was late when we got back, so the night attendant took Earl into one of the rooms and showed him which cot he could sleep in. He spotted one of his street-mates, greeting him with, "Hey, Ben, this guy runs the taxi from Old Orchard to Alfred. We just burned my fuckin' mum and brotha up." Earl stripped naked, and crawled under the mattress cover, falling asleep in under five seconds.

When I came in the next morning, I peeked into the room to see how Earl was doing and watched as Earl was awakened by the "chomp...slurp...crunch" of Ben loudly smacking down a bowl of Cheerios, sitting on Earl's mattress at the head of his bunk.

He slowly turned his head up toward Ben, who acknowledged his awakening by slowly nodding his head toward Earl, then continued to "chomp...slurp...crunch" until the little o's were all gone.

Earl stared curiously up at Ben as he finished the slurping and slobbering, and looked even more disgusted to see and hear Ben put the bowl to his lips and suck all the remaining milk from it, creating a high-pitched slurpy-whine as milk was sucked through his pursed lips, followed by a loud cheek popping belly bouncing belch. Apparently satisfied with his gastronomical performance, Ben slobbered the rest of the meal caught in his whiskers into his sleeve as he dragged it across his nose and mouth.

Earl cocked his head to the side, and looking a bit sick to his stomach said, "What's next? Maybe you gonna shit yer pants, eh?" Thinking of what Earl had just said, Ben got pissed off enough to tell Earl to go fuck himself, dropped the bowl on the floor, jumped to his feet losing his balance, and fell backwards on top of Earl.

As I walked into the room I saw Ben upside down with his legs turtling into the air, and naked little Earl pushing and pulling on pieces of Ben trying desperately to crawl out from under his thrashing self. Earl was yelling high-pitched obscenities suggesting Ben had been both ill-born and not well thought of by the deities. Ben was finally able to turn from his turtle position to one now facing and astraddle Earl, who squirmed and thrashed and grunted and groaned trying to rid himself of Ben's not well groomed and stinking body.

Earl and Ben arrived at the shelter within a couple weeks of each other, both in their early thirties, with long histories of hospitalization for schizophrenia, and now pretty much ignored by the mental health system, which maintained they were "not treatment compliant," and in need of unavailable resources, namely housing and support. Deinstitutionalization had pretty much trapped them, and a few million other poor and chronically mentally ill Americans, in a downward spiral from one-time care in the state hospital, to a broken promise from the emerging community mental health system.

As mentally ill people were moved out of the state hospitals, they were to be picked up and provided services in their home communities by the emerging community mental health centers. That worked pretty well for some of the people, but for those with severe and persistent mental illnesses, it has become synonymous with an early death. A low-income mentally ill person in Maine dies an average of twenty-five years sooner than the rest of the population.

Earl was able to eventually rid himself of a thrashing Ben, but neither he nor Ben would ever rid themselves of their mental illnesses, and neither would soon receive the kind of treatment and support they needed and were promised. They both remained on the shelter-shuffle circuit for another seven or eight years, after which we were able to place them in housing we had recently constructed. Combined, they were on the street and in the shelters for over forty years, and Ben died of neglect about eight years ago. Earl remains housed in a mental health center residential care facility, ever since that agency found out it could bill the government nearly four-hundred dollars a day for his care. He is now "treatment compliant."

Old Man and a Priest

Trying to escape the crush of a quarter of a million people, I charged down a tunnel escalator in the middle of the national mall and threw myself into one of the few available seats in a metro subway car. I'd just attended the 1988 rally on the great and fabled mall where 250,000 people had marched to demonstrate and lend support to the many celebrities and advocates for the homeless who'd come to underscore our demands that we provide affordable housing for the people who are so poor they have no place to live: "Housing Now."

It had been an inspirational and exciting event, which took over a year of planning to pull off, and as a member of the board of directors of the National Coalition for the Homeless, I was proud of the work they had done in organizing and coordinating with other Washington and national groups to make this such a success.

Throughout the afternoon, dozens of speakers described the worsening tragedy of too many thousands of our neighbors, trying to stay alive on the streets, in the alleys, and woodlots, and paltry number of emergency shelters patched together as token support for this too-long ignored group of citizens. Those wildly underfunded emergency shelters, springing out of church basements, and unused buildings, served as political cover for besieged politicians who not only didn't understand the killing dynamics of poverty, they didn't know what to do about it. There were those, additionally, who just didn't give a damn, and when confronted with the miserable reality of homeless bodies scattered about, found clever semantical ways of shifting the blame to the people who were homeless.

There seemed to be a growing sense across the land that, as President Reagan had once quipped, "They just want to be out there," and that extreme poverty is a choice, an enjoyable and relaxing way of life. The specter of that proverbial "welfare queen," forever buying lobster tails and wine with her endless supply of food stamps, and legions of food stamp recipients trading in their stamps for carloads of exotic South American drugs—which they sold, so they can sleep on a steaming metal grate outside the Museum of Science and Industry, gravel pits in Maine, or the lush landscaping surrounding millionaire condos in Florida—somehow mask the stark reality of women and children huddled under cardboard tents, hoping they'd not be beaten or raped again, as a man nearby chokes to death on his own vomit as delirium tremors end his miseries.

A major goal of this gathering was to offer up a more realistic flavor, smell, and feel to what it means to be homeless in the richest country in the world. Being poor is being without all of the things the rest of us take for granted, like nutritional food, ready access to health care, a safe and healthy place to live, and a role in helping to make our communities run more smoothly. Homelessness has nothing to do with all of that. To be homeless in America means to be hopeless in America, a position that forces a person to just quit imagining things could ever get much better, that what I have is what I have, period, and don't bother trying any longer to change it because no matter what, it isn't going to get any better.

At some point along this slide into oblivion, the use of adjectives becomes unnecessary when thinking of food, shelter, or health care—they either "are" or they "aren't." Words, like "nutritional, affordable, healthy, safe, affordable," are meaningless when they have nothing to qualify. Those things, absent hope, are things of the past. Life on the street is minute to minute, day to day, awaiting the inevitable, while learning to tolerate being beaten, raped, sick, cold, miserable, hungry, and made fun of.

The offensive behaviors of the homeless are not the cause of their extreme poverty. Those behaviors are the product of extreme poverty. If that were not true, most of us might occasionally qualify for admission into a homeless shelter. There is a tendency to imagine all homeless folks are the same, which is as foolish a notion as saying, "All Christians give a damn about the poor." It couldn't be further from the truth.

When I flopped into that metro seat back under the mall, I landed behind a Catholic priest, who seemed as if he, too, had just arrived, and was adjusting the overcoat under him when an old fellow dressed in a weathered, worn, and rumpled overcoat, tucked a newspaper under his arm, and plopped right down next to the priest. The priest, obviously not pleased with what he seemed to acknowledge as an intrusion into his space, roughly jerked his coat up and away from his seat-mate, snapping his head toward the window.

The old man, sporting a red-white-and-blue stocking hat, slowly unfolded his newspaper and began to read. The priest's body language betrayed his dislike of sitting next to the old man as his whole body seemed to stiffen and pull more and more away from him, mashing the priest closer to the window with each lurch of the train as it rumbled along.

After a short while, the old man lowered his paper and ever so gently nudged the priest with his elbow and asked, "Say, Father, what causes arthritis?"

The priest was visibly irritated by the touch and question and looking at his seatmate as though a bug had lit next to him, he gruffly bellowed, "Drunkenness, whoring around, and gluttony!" He then jerked his coat away from the old man, snorted, and resumed his out-the-window vigil.

The old man, who had gotten used to that sort of rebuff a long time ago, gently raised his newspaper and continued to read. After a few moments, I noticed a change in the priest's body language as his shoulders seemed to drop and his whole body settled into a more relaxed mood. Perhaps a butt-poke from On-High may have caused him to realize how abrupt and rude he had behaved toward the old man. He turned toward the old fellow and with his best "loving shepherd" smile, he kindly asked, "My son, how long have you had arthritis?" to which the old man slowly drawled, "Hell, Father, I ain't got arthritis. I's just reading here the Pope does."

The Poor

The Gospel takes away our right
forever, to discriminate between the
deserving and the undeserving poor.
—Dorothy Day

Somewhere in the middle of a sociology class at Drake University in the summer of 1964, it dawned on me that I had lived in poverty as a child. I at first resisted that notion and argued that the statistics being tossed about regarding family constellation, income, education, and social status were dribbled from the nose of an elitist asshole, trying to sell a textbook. Although both of my parents worked, we lived in a house, and had health insurance, my dad had only gone through eighth grade, and our family income fell out the bottom of a chart. Our family, consequently, was chucked into the "poor" bucket.

Over these decades, I've managed to not only accept that statistical fact, but have remained ever thankful nobody ever told us we were poor. It was just the way of life into which I was born that enabled, indeed, forced family and friends to work hard at staying connected and involved in each other's lives in an effort to survive. The sharing of food, buckets of coal, medicine, transportation, hand-me-down-clothes, and even rushing Christmas presents from one house to another on Christmas morning, meant that we were all an important part of keeping our collective boat afloat.

Being poor in America today is a whole different kettle of fish. First of all, society has devised various schemes to clearly label those who are poor with which come all the miseries of stigma and disrespect. Hospital charts epitomize the labelling process with words like "Medicaid, Indigent, General Assistance, County Aid, or Charity." A twenty-year-old female shelter guest taken to the emergency room for nausea and vomiting, on whose chart "Medicaid" was boldly stamped was mechanically asked by the physician as he came into the room, "How many pregnancies have you had?" It is somehow presumed that if you are poor, you are afflicted with bad things, like disease, dishonesty, and immorality.

Not unlike their more well-heeled counterparts, poor people sometimes do dumb things; sometimes take things that don't belong to them, suffer from addictions, are plagued with mental illness, and occasionally J-walk. Most of the widely heralded deviant behavior assigned to them, however, can be attributed directly to the poverty strangling the life from them, except the J-walking: that's inexcusable. Bad behavior does not create this poverty: it is the poverty which produces the bad behavior. There aren't, for instance, many rich people doing time in county jails.

Most of our family survived those times, grew up, had families, and each successive generation produces more college graduates, law enforcement officers, doctors, honest hard-working laborers, lawyers, and teachers. To our families' credit, as far as I know, we have not spawned a corporate CEO, hedge fund manager, or any other type of multi-millionaire hustler bent on getting as much as possible, no matter the cost.

All families, I suspect, have their own closet full of nasty little secrets, weird uncles, loud and rambunctious kids, and the black sheep n'er-do-well kid who stuns everybody by growing up and doing things universally known as "good," and so does ours. We even have a member here or there, struggling with financial woes, addictions, mental illness, and the legal entanglements that, from time to time, tend to accompany these maladies.

Few, if any of them, however, have ended up homeless, for several dramatic reasons: first of all, most of them are white; secondly, they still belong to a family that consciously pays attention to where they're at, how they're doing, and remains available to advocate on their behalf, when needed.

All of my friends in this little book came with lots of labels: drunk, junkie, pauper, nut-job, slacker, welfare cheat, queer, whore, hoodlum, boozer, druggie, lazy, bum, hobo, tramp, indigent, itinerant, transient, and whacko. They eventually figured out how to live with those demeaning tags as they went about the miserable business of just trying to stay alive, but were routinely jerked back into the reality of being poor as society systematically stapled one label after another to their asses while kicking them back to the curb.

Often, while advocating for justice and fair treatment of poor folks, elected officials, bureaucrats, philanthropists, church leaders, and the general public, while seeking to end the discomfort of having to deal with the issue and moment, will recite the biblical adage, "For the poor you will always have with you in the land." That said, the different congregants purse their lips, nod their heads approvingly, grunt, and go on home.

This old-saw recitation produces a shoulder-shrugging apathetic, hands in the air, metaphorical pat-on-the head, suggesting we tone down the revolutionary rhetoric and give up the fight to tackle poverty and injustice. And the damage is done, not unlike President Reagan's declaration that "they just want to be out there." What all of these good people are guilty of is hiding the truth—they either don't know or care enough about the subject to finish the quotation, "For the poor you will always have with you in the land. Therefore I command you 'You shall open wide your hand to your brother, to the needy and to the poor, in your land.'" (Deut. 15:7-11). "I command you."

About the Author

The best thing that happened to Donald H. Gean as a kid was that nobody ever told him he was poor. Absent the stigma and humiliation associated with this modern day and mean-spirited labelling ritual, he's been known all of his life as father, husband, teacher, administrator, advocate, and legislator. Not once did it occur to him he should even think about taking a seat on a back bench.

One-half of the proceeds from the sale of this book will be donated to the York County Shelter Programs in Alfred, Maine. The other half will help provide a home for two smiling old hippies.

CPSIA information can be obtained
at www.ICGtesting.com
Printed in the USA
BVHW080941221220
596004BV00001B/6